Praise for

The Hidden Journals

"This is a story about the time of transition, when the waves were just meeting the shore. You are reconnecting the hosted to the host. You have a story to tell, vastly different than the one commonly known."
CLIFFORD NAEOLE, Cultural Advisor, Maui

"I like the idea in this book that we must make space for other interpretations of these times. We have to transform history into light."
DR. JACK LOHMAN, Chief Executive Officer, Royal BC Museum

"Wade and Mary have written a story based on extensive research of original source material and oral stories encompassing both sides of the histories."
CASEY VANDEN HEUVEL, former Director, Squamish Lil'wat Cultural Centre

"A lot of our history is full of *na puka*. This could be a doorway, or holes in the story. I am very supportive of this book which is looking at the whole stories, based on original source material and oral stories, not just later interpretations."
CHI PILIALOHA, Museum Docent, Lahaina Restoration Foundation

"What Wade and Mary are writing is amazing. It is helping people connect. I feel that I know now why I exist because of this story."
DEBRA SPARROW, Coast Salish noble robe weaver

"The authors have been very persistent in finding the real stories of those times. It is particularly important information they have discovered about the gracious and respectful behaviours and manners of our royal women as described by Captain Vancouver. The true spirit of Kana Ka—humanity."
MA KUA SAM KAHA'I KAAI, Keeper of the Cultural Stories, Maui

"History is a collection of stories often written centuries after the facts, and based on interpretations. We must always consider the context of the times and what influences—religious, political or otherwise—may have set the tone for what is written. This story, based on years of archival research and previously unknown oral stories, will encourage people to think critically, ask questions and seek out alternative viewpoints."

JANE THORNTHWAITE, MLA, North Vancouver–Seymour, and former Chair, North Vancouver Board of Education

"This book is a refreshing delight to the senses, articulate and colourful. Primary records, images, oral stories, literary imagination and personal interviews come together seamlessly. The story is an exploration of the Baker family history on one hand, but also a reconsideration of history, another interpretation that provides a welcome alternative to official histories we have all grown up with in British Columbia. The authors reach beyond a critique of the past and the obvious injustice, and open up the historical imagination to portray a more dynamic and inclusive history between equals, based on respect and recognition of historical differences, sovereignty, and the establishment of relations based on reciprocity and protocol."

JOE DESJARLAIS, Principal, Northwest Trail Consulting, North Vancouver, BC

"I loved this book. WOW. I love PNW history, and everything said is true. I never stopped to wonder why we did not know more about that time, or about Captain Vancouver's interactions with the people he met. Thank you to both of you for doing the work and sharing it. This book is refreshing because it shows the struggles of a historian, and reminds us how history is interpreted and transformed into a narrative that is passed down. And if we don't stop to question it, we will perpetuate it."

TRACEY DRUM, teacher, Seattle, USA

"This book is a treat. It is so invigorating what your research has uncovered. You scratched below the surface, and found the core."

BONNIE WALKER, Lahaina Printsellers, Lahaina, Maui

The Hidden Journals

Captain Vancouver and His Mapmaker

A Personal Journey of Discovery

WADE BAKER & MARY TASI

Sky Spirit Studio Books
North Vancouver, BC

ISBN 978-0-9938438-1-5

Cataloguing in Publication data available from Library and Archives Canada

Book cover design: Wade Baker and Mary Tasi
Book interior design: Vivalogue Publishing (Canada) Limited

COVER IMAGES
Painting of HMS *Discovery* by Maurice Chadwick, 1992—
By permission of the Maritime Museum of BC
Photograph of Sierra Baker by Wilson Photography. Clothing by Touch of Culture.
Portrait of Lieutenant Joseph Baker, source unknown
Map of the Coast of Northwest America by Lieutenant Joseph Baker, 1798—
By permission of the Maritime Museum of BC

We gratefully acknowledge the financial support for research from the Province
of British Columbia through the First Peoples' Cultural Council.

Supported by
FIRST PEOPLES'
CULTURAL COUNCIL
Aboriginal Arts Development Awards

This book is based on factual and historical events; however, in some instances,
locales, names, details and identifying characteristics have been changed to
protect the privacy of individuals.

Printed in Canada

For our daughter, Sierra, and all the ancestors.
And for James Baker.

To: Kaci

In the spirit
of Capt Vancouver

Mary Tasi

Down in the deep, up in the sky,
I see them always, far or nigh,
And I shall see them till I die—
The old familiar faces.
And all day long, so close and near
As in a mystic dream I hear
Their gentle accents kind and dear—
The old familiar voices.
They have no sound that I can reach—
But silence sweeter is than speech.

Magnus and Morna
DINAH MARIA MULOCK CRAIK, 1876

"Humankind has not woven the web of life… we are but one thread within it. Whatever we do to the web, we do to ourselves. All things are bound together, all things connect…"

CHIEF SEATTLE OF THE SUQUAMISH

Acknowledgements

This book is dedicated with love and compassion to all the knowledge-keepers in British Columbia, England and Maui who shared their wisdom, traditions and oral stories with us. In some cases, they generously gave us hours and hours of their time to ensure that we had complete and accurate stories.

We would like to thank the Maritime Museum of BC in Victoria, particularly Anissa Paulsen, Curator/Collections Manager, and Judy Thompson. Judy went above and beyond to find missing files and documents, researching on her own time in London, England. Lea Edgar, the head archivist at the Vancouver Maritime Museum, permitted us to spend almost six months reading Captain Vancouver's original, edited 1798 journals, of which the museum has a copy.

Jane Thornthwaite, Member of the Legislative Assembly of British Columbia, North Vancouver–Seymour, is gratefully acknowledged for presenting this book to the Fourth Session, 40th Parliament, on July 13, 2015.

Debra Sparrow, Coast Salish noble robe weaver, generously shared her family ancestry. Debra Sparrow is descended from Khaltinaht, a granddaughter of the Chief George Capilano who met Captain Vancouver in 1792.

In Hawaii, Sam Kaha'i Kaai, cultural advisor and keeper of the knowledge, spent many days of his time sharing his encyclopedic knowledge of the late 18th century. Clifford Naeole, cultural advisor at The Ritz-Carlton hotel in Kapalua,

Maui, for over 20 years, also spent time with us, talking about the late 1700s, which he calls "the time of the to and fro."

Richard Mickelsen and Bryant Neal, directors of the Story of Hawaii Museum in Kapalua, shared their extensive knowledge of the Captain Cook/Captain Vancouver transition period, as well as the mapping routes that Captain Vancouver took on his journeys between the Pacific Northwest in America to the Sandwich Islands, as the Hawaiian Islands were known at the time. We particularly wish to thank the Lahaina Resoration Foundation in Lahaina, Maui, for connecting us with elders and allowing us to spend research time at the Hale Pa'i Museum.

In Vancouver, Nancy Nightingale generously contributed information about her father (and Wade Baker's uncle) Chief Simon Baker. Mary Point, director of the Musqueam Cultural Centre, was very supportive in giving us initial direction regarding Captain Vancouver's journals, which were purchased on their behalf by Alcan Aluminum. The contribution of Kilmeny Jane Denny was substantial. From editing the manuscript to emotional support and research suggestions, she was invaluable. Lynn Duncan from Vivalogue Publishing gave additional valuable suggestions and advice.

Prof. Jack Lohman, Chief Executive Officer of the Royal BC Museum, generously gave us access to his rare portrait of Captain Vancouver, as well as insight into Captain Vancouver's enigmatic character.

Dr. Nigel Rigby, Head of Research for the National Maritime Museum in Greenwich, England, gave us invaluable advice on the Lords of the Admiralty at the time, giving us his perspective about the missing documents, notes and journals.

John Lewis, Superintendent of Schools for the North Vancouver School District, read early drafts of the manuscript, and made many helpful suggestions.

Kevin Miller, former operations manager of the Harbourside Renaissance Hotel in Vancouver, gave us early support and ideas for the manuscript covers, thanks to his extensive interest and knowledge of early mapping in British Columbia. In addition, he hosted an information event for local historical societies at the hotel in January, 2015.

Captain Johann and the crew of the *Lady Washington* replica tall ship are gratefully acknowledged for giving us insight into the protocols of a tall ship of the late 18th century.

We would particularly like to thank the Joseph and Baker families in North Vancouver, and the Point and Sparrow families in Vancouver, who have been very supportive of our endeavours to bring these ancient oral records into the light. Many other elders shared stories as well, who have asked to remain anonymous.

Our good friend Tammy Chamberlayne graciously opened her homes on the Sunshine Coast to support the writing process.

We wish to acknowledge Neptune Bulk Terminals in North Vancouver for being the first to generously support the donation of this book to North Shore high schools.

There are many other persons, too numerous to mention, who gave support, critical advice and insight. They encouraged us to finish the book and "get it out to the world," so that people can read the whole story of those times. You all know who you are, and we are deeply grateful.

Contents

Preface

I n taking a journey of personal discovery and understanding, Wade Baker and Mary Tasi invite the reader to come aboard with a spirit of reflection, adventure and open curiosity.

What we readily accept as fact, upon further exploration is often revealed as myth, perpetuated through our lasting trust of the written word. We need to consider carefully the words that are written, hidden and omitted, for their intended meaning and purpose in selection. Are we being easily influenced and led to adopt a particular perspective of convenience, or are we prepared to examine multiple viewpoints to rediscover the "truth"?

Faced with oceans of information, teeming with bits of data among discarded debris, today's students are challenged to develop their critical thinking skills, to consider carefully their "facts" before reaching any definitive conclusions. Depending upon the perspective we take, or vantage point where we are situated, we will come to very different interpretations of what we will see, learn and know regarding the very same events in history.

The journey of discovery is often more important and revealing than the destination itself. Personal reflections in

The Hidden Journals, the original words of Lieutenant Joseph Baker and the rich storytelling of elders from generation to generation all engage the reader to broaden their perspective on their own personal ancestral journeys of discovery and understanding.

JOHN LEWIS

Superintendent of Schools

North Vancouver School District #44

North Vancouver, British Columbia

Canada

Introduction

This book is about Wade Baker's journey to discover a distant British ancestor from the late 1700s, a Royal Navy lieutenant named Joseph Baker, whom he had heard about as a child through oral storytelling.

Lieutenant Joseph Baker was a young officer and mapmaker on Captain George Vancouver's ship, HMS *Discovery*, and sailed with him on all his voyages from 1790 to 1795. A grant from the First People's Cultural Council in British Columbia in 2014 enabled further research for our story, including permission to access Joseph Baker's early logbooks and Captain Vancouver's journals.

This story interweaves primary source information with oral stories from elders in Maui and Vancouver. The oral stories were often almost identical to later findings in the journals and logbooks. This oral history filled in the gaps and missing pieces.

The Hidden Journals is a history story, but also a detective story. It shows the reader why museums and cultural centres need support, as there are fascinating documents, information and storytelling just waiting to be discovered. The reader will follow the authors' journey through Vancouver, Victoria, London (England) and Maui to uncover the true story of Captain Vancouver and his mapmaker, Lieutenant Joseph Baker.

As the research progressed, some interesting mysteries surfaced. We found out that Captain Vancouver's original, handwritten journals about his social relationships with the indigenous people he met are missing, as are some of the officers' journals. Soon after his death in 1798, Captain Vancouver's journals of his voyages were published, edited by his brother, John. The originals have disappeared.

In reading these 1798 journals in detail, a very different Captain Vancouver emerges than the one discussed in most 20th-century history books. This Captain Vancouver is a compassionate, high-level thinker, who is diplomatic and respectful with all the indigenous peoples he meets. He makes great friendships with the local kings and chiefs and their families, and he details the setting up of encampments on shore and extensive reciprocal social visits.

The protocol of these social and trading visits were often discussed at a first meeting on shore where a "line in the sand" was drawn: officers would sit on one side and the superior chiefs on the other. In the first of his journals, he writes:

May 22.d *1792* The canoes brought two superior chiefs, attended by about five others, about two hundred yards off the ship, and there—resting on their paddles, a conference was held, followed by a song principally sung by one man, who at times was joined in chorus by several others, whilst some in each canoe kept time with the handles of their paddles by striking them against the gunwale or side of the canoe. This formed a sort of accompaniment, a most agreeable effect. This performance took place whilst they were paddling slowly around the ship, and on its being concluded, they came alongside with the greatest confidence, and without fear or suspicion immediately entered into a commercial transaction with our people... they uniformly had a decided preference for copper, and the trading was conducted in a very fair and honest manner... They conducted themselves with the utmost propriety and neither the ladies or children ventured on board... two days later accompanied by Mr. Baker in the yawl, we set out to examine the area.[1]

This is just one example of what we discovered had been excised from modern history—the real story of the relationships between Captain Vancouver, his crew and the indigenous peoples they met on their journey of discovery at the end of the 18th century.

The Hidden Journals charts our fascinating voyage of discovery into the authentic story of Wade's ancestor, Lieutenant Joseph Baker, and his captain, George Vancouver, on their travels to the northwest coast of Canada and the islands of Hawaii, 1792–1795.

CHAPTER 1

Chilliwack, British Columbia, 1967

That is our mountain.

DANIEL BAKER

That's our mountain," said my father, pointing to Mount Baker. Over the horizon, the white, snow-capped mountain majestically beckoned to us, an ancient volcano waiting to erupt.

The whole family was going to the summer Salish war canoe races at Cultus Lake. We were driving in our family Dodge station wagon. Dad was driving, Mum was sitting silently in the passenger seat and my twin brother Wayne and I were seated behind. Pam and Darlene were in the rumble seat in the back, facing the rear, talking about fashions and hairstyles, the usual. That Dodge station wagon had a roof rack and fake wood panel siding along the side. It was a pretty cool car for the times, the very first car with push-button windows.

It was a nice hot summer day, family time. Dad loved going to the canoe races as he would catch up on all the gossip from the different clans and tribes along the coast. I was probably around 11 years old. My twin and I were only interested in thinking about which girls may be at the lake. It seemed to me that no one was really listening to Dad. No one questioned or answered him. Oh, Dad's making a big deal of something, I thought, something we had no interest in.

Daniel and Emily Baker, circa 1950

He continued driving, silently gazing at the mountain, staring ahead, his hands on the steering wheel, waiting for one of us to say something, it seemed. He seemed disappointed by the lack of response, and sombrely drove for awhile, deep in thought.

Thinking back now, I wish I would have listened more to something he was trying to teach us about our lineage, our legacy. He realized we were too young, and that we had our own future ahead...

As he spoke, I vaguely remembered hearing something at Grannie Lizzie's bedside. She was my great-grandmother.

My Dad only took us twins as I recall. I was seven years old then. Wayne had run off outside to play with the cousins and I was at Grannie Lizzie's bedside. She looked at least 100 years old. In her room, there were empty seats for company during the day and empty seats for the spirits who would visit in the evenings.

Grannie Lizzie seemed ancient and old, and old people scared me. They seemed to know about so many shamanic things that we did not talk about at home.

"What is left is best left unsaid," I heard. I stood and leaned against the wall. I did not want to sit on those chairs that the ghosts sat on.

Suddenly their voices lowered, and I strained to hear them. I heard Grannie Lizzie talking about a third lieutenant again.

"I know I am leaving this world," she said. "Dan, can you please keep this little bit of our history alive, maybe for someone to write about it in the future?"

Perhaps Dad had a premonition that at least one of us may look into this story when we were older, look into our roots. I had no idea that, in the future, my wife and I would be the ones recording this story of two worlds that merged in the long ago past. I wish I had listened more carefully to the stories my parents told me about our family and previous generations. We missed opportunities to learn a great deal more from our ancestors by not listening at the time to the storytelling, passed down from generation to generation.

And then I forgot about this for a long, long time.

CHAPTER 2

Maui, 2008

History has its own true rhythm.
SAM KAHAʻI KAAI

Christmas Eve, my daughter and I were sitting eating shaved ice under the banyan tree in Lahaina, waiting for Mary. She had gone to visit the Baldwin House Museum on Front Street. She would always visit museums and cultural centres when we travelled.

All the tourists were in the shops looking for Christmas presents, enjoying the street theatre and the parade of multicultural people on Front Street, many wearing leis and flowers in their hair, revelling in the warm tropical breeze. There was a sense of escape from the usual annual duties of days of food shopping and turkey preparation, and being trapped in cold houses with overbearing relatives.

We finally saw Mary walking towards us, an air of frustration surrounding her. She sat down and shared this story with us:

THE BALDWIN HOUSE MUSEUM, the oldest house still standing on Maui, was almost deserted. I went inside and a tall and lanky man approached me, glad to have a visitor.

"Would you like a tour of the house?' he asked me pleasantly. "This was the Reverend Dwight Baldwin's home. He also served as doctor, veterinarian and dentist. This was the doctor's house, and it was built earlier." I followed him with interest as he pointed out the living spaces, period furniture and various others items of a doctor's family life and practice in the early 1800s.

"So, there is a chance that Lt. Joseph Baker may have visited here?" I asked. "Oral history I have received from elders is that he had a son he left in Vancouver, and also here on Maui. There are many Hawaiian Bakers, correct?"

The man looked at me condescendingly. "Oh. No, the officers stayed on the ship. There was no socializing with the locals," he said with one of those haughty Boston accents.

"You actually believe those young and handsome Royal Navy officers stayed on the ship for three years of winter visits?" I asked him incredulously. Then I realized we were about to have a full-out argument on Christmas Eve, so I abruptly decided to leave the museum. He was so set in his prejudices. There was no way I was going to convince him. However, it did make me realize how easily history can be distorted one way or another to suit the bias of the storyteller, or the prevailing prejudices or agendas of the times.

WHAT MARY HAD shared made me realize that we needed to find out some more information. I recalled my sister Pam telling me that she remembered Dad trying to tell her something when we were in Maui on a family trip in the late 1960s.

"I think he wanted to go into a museum to show us something," she said, "but we had no interest."

The next day Mary and I stepped off the Maui Island bus and strolled into the Whaler's Village outdoor shopping centre in Kaanapali Bay, looking for a late afternoon snack. We walked by a store, then backtracked. Its sign said LAHAINA PRINTSELLERS ANTIQUE AND VINTAGE HAWAIIAN MAPS. Perhaps there may be something here, we thought.

We walked in, and a very friendly and personable middle-aged lady with blond hair approached us. "Can I help you?" she asked. "My name is Bonnie, and I manage this store."

"We are looking for any maps or information about Lt. Joseph Baker," Mary said.

Bonnie listened intently to our story about how we could find little to no information about Lt. Baker in Vancouver.

Then she said, "Sure, I have his original lithographs here." She bent down, opened a low cabinet drawer and pulled out a large lithograph.

This is amazing, I thought. Bonnie sold us several small reproduction maps at a 50 percent discount.

"His original lithographs are here. They are 8,000 dollars," she said. Bonnie looked at us as if she was wondering if we had that kind of money for an ancestor's map.

"I can give you some discount," she said. We politely declined, however.

I was astonished to see maps of the Sandwich Islands (Hawaii) and Vancouver Island drawn by "Joseph Baker,

Third Lieutenant." That was the first time I had seen his name in print. The name that I remembered hearing at Grannie Lizzie's bedside. I suddenly had a feeling that there was more to this story that my Dad would talk about on those trips to Cultus Lake. This hit a chord with me: there was another family branch of the Baker clan, and perhaps there was some credence to Dad's story.

Bonnie also let us leaf through a book she had on the back table called *Early Mapping of Hawai'i* by Gary L. Fitzpatrick. There was an excerpt that caught our eye.

Captain Vancouver's voyage resulted in the first published map of Hawai'i to depict the islands in their entirety. Although the chart is credited to Lt. Joseph Baker, it likely represents the work of several men. Until 1876, these maps were the primary source of information. No subsequent navigators spent as much time in Hawai'i, or cruised as much of the ocean. Baker's chart is probably one of the most significant in Hawaiian history.[2]

CHAPTER 3

Vancouver Research, 2009

*We are taught to believe that the Great Spirit sees
and hears everything, and that he never forgets,
that hereafter he will give every man a spirit home
according to his desserts… This I believe, and all
my people believe the same.*

CHIEF JOSEPH OF THE NEZ PERCE

W hen we came home, I started researching with all the new technology resources of Wikipedia and Google. I typed in the name "Lieutenant Joseph Baker" and "Her Majesty's ships," and suddenly there was a lot of overwhelming information.

The Wikipedia entry said: "Joseph Baker, 1767 to 1817, was an officer in the Royal Navy, best known for his role in the mapping of the Pacific Northwest Coast of America during the Vancouver Expedition of 1791 to 1795. Mt. Baker is named after him."

Joseph Baker was the second son of James and Nancy Baker, born in 1768 in Bristol, in the southwest of England.

A second son had to make his own way in the world, as British tradition at the time only allowed first sons to inherit the family estates and business interests. It is likely the Baker family had interests in wool trading and textile businesses.

Mary and I found only one book on the internet about Joseph Baker, written by Robert C. Wing. We promptly ordered two copies of *Joseph Baker: Lieutenant on the Vancouver Expedition*, one for us and one for my mother.

When we gave the book to my mother, she said, looking at the picture on the cover, "Is that him?"

We said, "Yes, but at a much older age. When he was here he would have been around 24."

Wing's book is well researched and covers the various voyages of Joseph Baker, his promotion from third lieutenant to first lieutenant, and his subsequent career as the captain of his own ship, the *Tartar*, "assigned to what is now Latvia and Estonia, as far north as the gulf of Finland."[3] The book also includes letters from Baker's court martial on October 23, 1811, after he accidentally grounded his ship on the island of Dago. I read about his mapping and his later, retired life in Presteigne, Wales, with his British wife, Elizabeth, to whom he was married for 20 years, from 1797 to his death in 1817.

My ancestor must have thoroughly enjoyed the seafaring life, as he continued to request sea duty after his marriage, and was gone for long periods of time. Even so, he managed to have eight children with Elizabeth.

I was now thinking: I have relatives in England I have never met. And then I found his will on the internet. He wrote it shortly after his marriage to Elizabeth, two years after he returned home from his voyages with Captain Vancouver and before they had any children. Written just before Baker left for sea for another voyage, it said: "Due to my transitory life, I want to avoid any controversies after my decease." He left everything to his British wife.

Unfortunately, I did not print this off the internet at the time, and it has now disappeared from open public view. In 2014, Judy Thompson of the Maritime Museum of BC in Victoria found us a copy of Lt. Baker's 1790 will, obtained from the National Archives in Kew, England.

I, Joseph Baker, midshipman, of His Majesty's Ship Discovery, being in bodily health and of sound and disposing mind and memory, and considering the perils and dangers of the seas, and other uncertainties of this transitory life (do for avoiding controversies after my decease) make, publish and declare this my last Will and Testament in manner following (That is to say) First, I recommend my soul to God that gave it, and my Body I commit to the Earth or Sea as it shall please God to order, and as for and concerning all my worldly Estate, I give, bequeath and dispose thereof as followeth. That is to say, after payment of my just debts and funeral Expenses all such...

Wages, Sum and Sums of money, lands, tenements, Goods, Chattels, and Estate whatsoever, as shall be any ways due owing or belonging unto me at the time of my decease, I do give, devise and bequeath the same unto my friend Captain James Vashon of the Royal Navy.

And I do hereby nominate and appoint Edward Ommanney and John Page of Bloomsbury, Lord of..., *executors of this my last Will and Testament, hereby revoking all former and other wills, Testaments and Deeds of*

Gifts by me at any time heretofore made. And I do ordain and ratify these Presents to stand and be for, as my only last Will and Testament

In Witness to this my said Will, I have set my Hand & Seal the Second Day of March in the Year of our Lord One Thousand Seven Hundred and Ninety And in the Thirtieth year of the Reign of his Majesty King George the Third over Great Britain & c.

Signed, sealed, published and declared by Joseph Baker.

The story of Lt. Joseph Baker's relationship with a daughter of Chief Capilano who became one of his wives, is not in Wing's book. Later, when researching the Vancouver Expedition's naval "Observations of the Day," I saw that there were only mentions of visiting villages and the social relationships with royal kings and chiefs. Baker's marriage to Chief Capilano's daughter is an oral story, handed down through my family.

I became very excited and curious. Our relatives in England have no idea, I thought. I would often meet tourists from England as part of my ambassador work at Klahowya Village in Vancouver's Stanley Park, and they would say, "We know nothing in England about what transpired over here with those early explorers. We are not taught anything about it in the schools—just the technical aspects of the voyages and mapping. Of course, there must be more to the stories. They were away for years."

I couldn't find anything on the internet or in books about my ancestor's relationship with the First Nations. It is as if there were orders not to talk too much about the indigenous peoples they encountered. Lt. Baker's job was just to take care of the "people," discipline the deckhands and officers, and organize the sails on the ship. Keep the crew busy, there were to be no idle hands, is my feeling.

My eldest brother, Dennis, told me one day as we were having coffee at the Lonsdale Blenz in North Vancouver, "Oh, the government did not want any stories about the connections between those English officers and the natives. They changed the stories."

One hot August day in Stanley Park in 2014, a passing Coast Salish elder told Mary and me a story. We had started chatting to her about this book, and she suddenly sat down on the chair next to our cultural booth in the shade of the cedar trees. She started talking:

"OH, THEY WERE full of piss and vinegar, like any young men. They thought, I will come back to England in 20 years and show my family. I am the second or third son that was sent off to the colonies and had to make my own way. They were often the black sheep. A lot did not go back. England at the time was filthy, sewage in the streets. They came here and it was paradise. They needed that native woman to survive. They did not know how to shoot. Oh, maybe they had a shooting club in England. They knew nothing about these big tides; oh, maybe they had a little pond stocked with trout on their estate. In some cases, it was an honour to have the chief's daughter marry these guys, they were maybe... Oh, be careful saying that... I know there is not a lot out there... it is awkward. That is all I am going to tell you. I have to go now—don't you use my name now."

She gave us a hard stare. Then, as she left, she turned back towards us. Mary was still furiously scribbling down her words on a scrap piece of paper. With a half smile, the elder said, "Mary, you and Wade better get this book finished quick," and she left, her silver whale earrings sparkling in the late afternoon sun.

IN 2012, I went back to school and my year-end presentation was about this story, a story that the Squamish Nation and the people were never able to talk about. It was a challenge for me to step up and show this story in a visual way. For the longest time, this was all hush-hush, because of the shame the Church had ingrained in us. They made us feel that mixed blood was shameful—then called half-breed—and that it was not accepted in either the First Nations or Caucasian world for political reasons, I now see.

I stood on the middle of the fence for the longest time. To get off this fence, I had to talk about this story to break the spell put onto us by the Church, with its own agendas to promote a false cultural identity. I started researching more, reading Lt. Joseph Baker's logbooks and the journals of Captain Vancouver.

And I talked to Walter Joseph.

CHAPTER 4

North Vancouver Oral Stories

*Through calm and storm, we shall sail, guided by
the voices of our ancestors.*
CLIFFORD NAEOLE

Walter Joseph is my neighbour, cousin and good friend. He is a keeper of the stories. Certain individuals in the tribe have that gift, that ability to retain all the information from the past, taught to them so they can teach the exact and whole histories to the new generation. We are as close as brothers. In our way, the Bakers and the Josephs are brothers. Grannie Lizzie lived with them for awhile—the Josephs took care of her in her old age.

Walter also spoke to Mary one day outside our Sky Spirit Studio, on Chief Joseph Crescent in North Vancouver.

"I was walking into the studio when I saw Walter Joseph riding by on his bicycle," Mary said. "I asked him, 'May I speak to you for a moment? We are writing a story about Wade's ancestor, Lt. Joseph Baker. Can you tell me again

A PERSONAL JOURNEY OF DISCOVERY

what you know about it?' Walter went into computer mode, bringing out precise memories, as if he was present at the moment."

Walter said, "My great-grandmother was Elizabeth Joseph (maiden name Baker). Grannie Lizzie's father was John Baker, her mother was an Indian name, Mary Tsilyaliya Baker.

e 2A   The Citizen, Wednesday, May 12, 1971

CENTURY-OLD FACE of Mrs. Lizzie Jacobs, of 225 Lawa Avenue, on the Capilano Reserve. Mrs. Jacobs, widow of well-known Chief Jacobs, lives with grand-daughter Mrs. Yvonne Joseph.

Grannie Lizzie taught at Gibson's school over on the Sunshine Coast. I remember seeing a photo of her wearing a big hat. She used to talk about a third lieutenant all the time. Her grandfather or great-grandfather, she said. I believe he came back from England and stayed in Stanley Park for awhile with them. Eleven years after Lt. Baker was first here, he came back to see his second wife whose children became the Josephs, he was so in love with her. The women were beautiful here. There was a bad connotation, a smear campaign, saying that a later John Baker was a ship jumper. It was not true. It was all made up so the government could take Stanley Park and remove us from our lands."

Mary told him about the logbooks, the journals and how Captain Vancouver had described the European features and light olive skin of the indigenous people he had met. And the smallpox marks.

"Yes, the Spanish came through first with their diseases," he said.

Mary said, "Walter, can Wade and I take you out for lunch to talk more about this?"

"Oh, it would take a lot more time than a lunch. They are changing ancient history everywhere, putting bad connotations on things."

"Walter had finished sharing," Mary told me. "He jumped on his mountain bike and rode off."

I later asked Walter if he could write any of this down. He looked up in the sky, and said he had to ponder about that.

I could see his mind was like an encyclopedia, the oral history always present, as if he was there in the time frame. Mary said it reminded her of her great-aunts and grandmothers in

Hungary, how they would talk and argue of ancient times as if it was last week. I realized the anger and frustration was still close to the surface, as Walter got older, the past became even closer, waiting to be resolved.

IN VANCOUVER, DEBRA SPARROW, Coast Salish noble robe weaver, became very interested in this story after seeing our presentation panels about our project. One photo showed the unnamed portrait of a Coast Salish superior chief's daughter, which I had found on the internet, and had a jolt of recognition when I saw it. We were leaning on a glass case at the Musqueam Cultural Centre museum talking about this book.

"Is that her?" Debra exclaimed. She had noticed the small portrait of the striking young lady, next to the painting of Joseph Baker that I had used in my school presentation.

"Yes, I know it is her, I feel it," I said.

"What is her name?" Debra asked.

"We don't know."

"Do you have any ideas? She looks like Khaltinaht, the first wife of Portuguese Joe. Khaltinaht is my ancestor from the mid-1850s."

Debra turned sideways from Mary and me, and swept the curtain of long black hair back from her face. We both stared at her profile.

"You look exactly like her!" Mary and I exclaimed at the same time. It was unmistakeable. The three of us stared at each other, speechless, caught in a moment where the past had suddenly bumped straight into the present, as if a portal had opened. We were honoured with a glimpse of a moment from long ago. "We need to talk more about this," Debra said.

We arranged to meet a week later at the Cornerstone Café on Stephens Street in Vancouver. Debra walked in wearing a flowing aqua scarf with her own salmon crest designs printed on the scarf. She sat down after ordering a lemonade and started speaking.

"Khaltinaht was one of Chief Capilano's granddaughters from a much later marriage. Khaltinaht would have lived about 60 years after the young lady we are looking for. Chief Capilano had many wives; no one wants to speak of this."

Debra had brought a new book about Portuguese Joe and his Coast Salish family with her. Portuguese Joe Silvey was born in Portugal and came to the West Coast on a whaling schooner in 1860. He married Khaltinaht, the granddaughter of Chief Capilano. However, she died after a few short years of marriage, and Joe married his second wife, Kwatleematt (Lucy), who was from the Sechelt First Nation. He had a total of 11 children with the two women.

Debra opened *Shore to Shore* by Suzanne Fournier, the book she had brought with her. She pointed out the picture of her ancestor, Khaltinaht, who was wearing a beautiful headdress of dentalium shells and a traditional Coast Salish woven robe embellished with her family crests. All Khaltinaht's regalia denoted her rank and highborn status as a granddaughter of Chief Capilano. She had attractive, soft, feminine features and an intelligent air. The marriage of Khaltinaht to Portuguese Joe would have been celebrated at a traditional mask ceremony at the chief's longhouse, Debra explained.

Could it be possible that Lt. Joseph Baker's marriage to Khaltinaht's great-aunt was celebrated with exactly this same type of ceremony? Their alliance would have been a formal one, we all agreed. It is not possible that they would have just lived together secretly. The behaviour and actions of an unmarried, superior chief's daughter at that time (1792–1795) would have been highly regulated, with strict protocols. An unsanctioned relationship between an outsider and a highborn princess would have resulted in death or severe punishment.

It suddenly became so important to the three of us to find out her name. She had lived so briefly, and likely passed away from pneumonia at the age of 17 or 18. Perhaps she had been sick with concern about whether Joseph Baker was ever coming back to see her and their babies, after he left to continue the voyage to the Sandwich Islands (Hawaii).

We told Debra that many elders had spoken to us, but some did not want their names used in our book.

"You can use my name," Debra said. "I am so pleased that you and Mary are doing this work."

Debra told us that her great-great-grandmother, Hulimia, was the youngest of ten brothers and sisters from one of Chief Capilano's wives. He had two wives from the Musqueam community in Vancouver, then moved to the North Shore (North Vancouver) and took at least two more Coast Salish wives from that area. He built his longhouse and homestead on the banks of the Capilano River. Multiple marriages were very common in those times across indigenous cultures. It had the practical benefit of creating alliances with other tribes, and ensuring that enough healthy children were born to continue the line of nobility. It was only later that this practice became shameful, due to the missionaries' insistence on a Christian marriage ceremony, where only one wife was entered into the records.

This royal daughter to whom Joseph Baker was attracted was likely very special. The elders would watch the young children, noting the one or two amongst them who had a wisdom beyond their years, and who could learn rapidly. It is very likely that this princess may have spoken a few words of Spanish, as the Spanish explorer José María Narváez had arrived in Point Grey in 1791, bringing native interpreters with them.

Chief Capilano was very wise and he knew the value and importance of setting up royal alliances for his favourite daughters with other tribal chiefs to ensure peace and prosperity. It would have been seen as an asset to create an alliance with the British officers, who would have been seen as highborn and well connected to the powerful nations to the east. Once you are family, the community is safe. They knew this new world was coming: the Spanish had been there the year before.

Then Debra said, "The important question is, who brought who to whom?"

Did the young princess bring Lt. Joseph Baker to her father, or vice versa?

"It seems very likely it was a strong love relationship," said Mary. "Anyone who remembers falling deeply in love at 14 or 15 will attest to that. Joseph was 24, unmarried and would have been very handsome in his lieutenant's uniform."

I believed my ancestor had an open-minded and adventurous personality. It is possible that this was a very strong, committed relationship for the two young people, not the stereotype of a passing, casual attraction, as presented by 20th-century historians, writing from their own prejudices.

Possibly a likeness of Kwasan, Princess Capilano. Artist unknown

All the oral evidence we were uncovering pointed to the fact that yes, this was a very strong relationship, a fact that was buried because it did not serve the political agenda of the times.

Debra told us later, after some thoughtful discussions with her family, that she felt this young lady's name could have been Kwasan, meaning "Star" or "Noble Star." Debra told us that Portuguese Joe called his boat *Morning Star*, likely after his first wife Khaltinaht, and that Coast Salish legends state that our spirits "are in the stars."

So, Kwasan was what we agreed to call the Coast Salish princess who married Lt. Joseph Baker in this story. This is the anglicized version of her name. The Coast Salish Peoples are a group of ethnically and linguistically related indigenous people of the Pacific Northwest Coast, in British Columbia, Canada, and the states of Washington and Oregon in the United States.

Debra encouraged us to keep writing. She told us how she called on her late grandfather to help her, saying, "You had better come with me and bring those writers from the other side, those writers from the other world to help me. Otherwise, others will write books about us, without our true stories. We have the fine thread of the oral tradition moving through us. I already know this information. I can feel it from my ancestor's DNA."

What Debra was talking about was the exact same thing as what Mary had experienced with her ancestral memories from ancient Hungarians, and which she wrote about in her book, *Spirit Memory*.

"My Grandpa can now rest in peace as I have connected into the millennia of storytellers. Three hundred years of our stories are now being passed down through me. First the stories were told in the canoes, then in the horse and buggies, and now in cars and coffee shops. Mary, in your story *Spirit Memory*, the man in that antique shop said to you, 'Know who you are and where you come from,' when he gave you that copper box with the seven Hungarian chieftains embossed on top.[4] Remember that scene as you write this story with Wade. A politician from Ottawa once said, 'I do not see signs on the mountaintops that the native people own this land.' Well, I say that 10,000 years of our ancestors are buried in this ground, all you have to do is look, and hear the stories they are telling us."

IN COAST SALISH and Kwakiutl tradition, there is the witness ceremony. Everything of importance is witnessed by the community. At least four people are called forward and are given a traditional gift to ensure that they will pass on what they have witnessed that day. In modern day, they are given a quarter each, as well as other gifts depending on the importance of the occassion. The marriage of Lt. Joseph Baker and Kwasan would have been witnessed, and the oral stories were passed down to this day. Their story is finally being told, so that this young couple can have the respect they deserve for defying convention and preserving their relationship through the children that were conceived.

MY MOTHER, CHIEF Emily Nelson Baker, shared her recollections with us about her life and protocols for a superior chief's daughter.

"My mother was descended from Robert Hunt and Mary Ebbit, daughter of an Alaskan superior chief, Chief Ebbits, on her mother's side. Her mother's great-grandfather, Robert Hunt, was from England, one of those second or third sons of nobility who were sent to the New World to add to the family fortunes. He managed the Pacific Coast fur trade route for the Hudson's Bay Company, and was the chief factor at the Fort Rupert Trading Post.

"Mary Ebbit was an Alaskan high chief's daughter. Robert Hunt met her in Alaska, while on business for the Hudson's Bay Company. They married and had 12 children, whose descendants are now all renowned artists and historians. All the children were home-tutored and received an excellent education. Robert was offered the Fort Rupert Hudson's Bay Trading Post to manage and they became one of the founding families of the area."

Mary and I found pictures of Mary Ebbit and Robert Hunt in antique books, but none showing them together. We have a picture of them standing side by side. Mary is wearing a Victorian gown with a high collar, and Robert has the classic, long sideburns fashionable in the mid-1850s. They look like a high status, proud and respectable couple, along with their friends Governor James Douglas and his Irish-Cree wife, Amelia Douglas. Governor Douglas wrote proudly of his wife: "Darling good mama was nicely got up and won all hearts with her kindness and generosity."[5]

My mother Chief Emily Nelson Baker was born in 1921 in Alert Bay. Her father, Alex Nelson, was a highly ranked hereditary chief of the Musgamagw Dzawadaenuxw, a group of four tribes. Her mother was Grace Hunt, from the Kwakiutl Nation, a group of tribes who encompass most of the northwest coast of British Columbia. Her mother was Grace

Hunt, her mother's father was David, her grandfather was George Hunt.

"The first generation of Hunt women all married white guys, and all those government men in Victoria married native women. Where are all those children now? I don't see them at the potlatches. My mother, Grace, could pass as a white woman and she loved school. She wanted to go to the local public girls school—she ran away to school, and her mother went and brought her home. My parents divorced when I was young. My mother told me that my father's family was very hard on her, that is probably the reason they split up."

When Emily was seven years old, she was sent to St. Michael's Residential School in Alert Bay. On Saturdays, she was allowed to visit relatives. On Sundays, she would go to a little church in the village called St. George's. When she was older, she would go to afternoon dances at the church with her sister. She was very protected and not allowed out after dark. She met her future husband, Daniel Baker, at one of the dances. Daniel was from Vancouver and was fishing up in the Alert Bay area. He asked her mother's permission if he could marry Emily and bring her to Vancouver. It was a strong love relationship, and they later had seven children together. There was a Council of Elders convened, because Emily had been named chief by her father at her birth, and it was very important to the tribe what happened to her.

My mother told us the story of her birth.

"My mother was in labour in Alert Bay. My father, his parents and grandparents, uncles and aunties were all outside the house, waiting for me to be born. My father made an announcement he would step down from his position, regardless of whether the baby was a male or female. 'The baby will stand in my position,' he announced to the gathering. He made this announcement to everyone present, to all the forefathers.

Chief Lucy Emily Nelson Baker, aged 3, 1924, Fort Rupert, BC

"They never even asked me if I wanted it or not. I wasn't even born yet!"

To explain what she meant by "position," my mother went into the back bedroom and brought out some papers to show us. There were pages and pages of names and tribes. At the very top of the first page, Kwee-k-Eagle Clan, was listed as one of her clans. She has several native names to show her prominence and status.

"Our clan was Number One, above all the clans, you could say. My father, Alex Nelson, was next in line to inherit from Chief Dick Webber. He had four 'seats' or four hereditary chieftainships. Our family had four coppers representing this, which disappeared during the banning of the potlatches. The four Chieftainships are:

> Kwikw Seat
> LilaWagila Clan
> Wayu'kwama'yi Clan
> Gigalgam Clan

"My father passed away before Chief Webber, and I was named next in line for the 'position.' I have hosted four potlatches, two feasts and donated to many causes including helping to rebuild the Alert Bay longhouse after the fire. However, some people don't want to recognize my inherited status at times for political reasons. Yet, this has been documented by the Royal British Columbia Museum in Victoria. They have documents from George Henry who was the last known Nameskeeper among the clans. His job was to remember the order of social rank. I have the rights to all the dances, songs and masks from these four hereditary chieftainships. Are you writing this all down correctly, Mary?"

The elders agreed that it was better to send her away, a highly unusual decision as marriages were still being arranged at that time. Emily told me the elders agreed to her going to Vancouver as they felt there was extreme jealousy of her in the community, and it was better to remove her from it.

"There was 'bad medicine' in the community called Ee-Ka. I was told not to throw away an apple core after eating it, as someone with malicious intent could pick it up and place Ee-Ka on me. Malicious intent starts with intense jealousy, then becomes malicious intent when several people with powerful negative energies come together."

Daniel and Emily Baker, Granville Street, Vancouver, 1951

My mother, Lucy Emily, was the daughter of a superior chief and named a chief at birth. Some in the community felt she had unfair favouritism, as she had not suffered like some others at residential school because of her fair skin and blond hair, passed down to her from Robert Hunt. Her nickname at school was "Blondie," and she was allowed to go home and visit relatives in Alert Bay on weekends.

My father, Daniel, was unfortunately sent to one of the worst residential schools in British Columbia. He and his brothers were sent to St. George's Residential School in Lytton, far from home to discourage visitors. They tried to run away several times, and were always caught and brought back by one of the Indian agents. An elder from Lytton told me that he remembers the preteen boys running away, and then brought back, pulled behind horses with ropes around their necks.

My cousin, Nancy Nightingale, told me. "The first time they ran away they hitchhiked and got rides to Vancouver from Fraser Canyon. The second time they borrowed a canoe at Boston Bar, and paddled for two days to get to North Vancouver. Daniel was the youngest and tired easily, so his brothers Bill, James and Simon took turns piggybacking him. They slept on an island to escape notice, and when they awoke, they were covered in harmless garden snakes. The island is still called Snake Island.

"My father, Simon, was a leader at the school and managed to get all the children to declare they would not work in the fields until palatable food was served to them. His brother James died from an untreated illness at the school as the priests refused to call a doctor. The head priest told Simon he had to force his brother's body to fit into the coffin, which was made for a much younger child."

Daniel, my father, never spoke of his experiences at the school to me and my brothers and sisters.

Many Canadians do not know that allegedly half of the children sent to residential school never returned to their families. They died from malnutrition, untreated illnesses and murder. By law at that time, they were not allowed to attend public schools. Some of the schools were still operating in the early 1990s. In my opinion, there needs to be memorials at all the school sites to honour these children.

In April 2014, Mary and I visited my father's former residential school chapel in Lytton. We climbed the stairs and pushed open the door to the church. There were several deadbolts, but it was not locked and the rusted door opened easily with a slight push. Grey dust coated the altar, the benches and the floor. Jewelled pieces of stained glass from the high, broken windows were scattered around the floor. Prayer books were still strewn everywhere, and the pillows the priests had knelt on were still here, forgotten. It was as if no one had been inside for 50 years. I saw a large plaque on the west wall and walked over to it.

I read out loud:

This tablet records that the Institute of St. George's Lytton was founded in 1901 under the Trusts of the Company for the propagation of the Gospel in New England and the ports adjacent in America called the NEW ENGLAND COMPANY. By Agreement with the Department of Indian Affairs of the DOMINION OF CANADA, the Buildings, Estates and Management were handed over by the aforesaid company to the Government of CANADA in 1927.

Nothing on the plaque mentions education. It was very clear this was a business arrangement and I needed to research the political agenda behind it.

In 2007, settlement cheques for residential school survivors began being mailed out as a minimal compensation. In 2011, the Truth and Reconciliation Commission was established by the Federal Government. My mother had to prove which residential school she had attended, by a photo or some other means.

"They told me they had no record of me attending that school, so luckily I had a class photo to show them," she said. She pointed herself out in the photo on her wall. I thought how much our daughter, Sierra, looked like her grandmother at that same age.

My mother told me when she went to the government office on Esplanade in North Vancouver to pick up the residential school settlement cheque, the lady asked her what she was most upset about.

"For one, I missed out on my culture," she told her.

"I did not want to take that cheque, but then I took it and used it towards buying back at Maynard's auction house our family chilcat robe that Mary Ebbit wove in the 1850s. I outbid that buyer from a New York museum. When I was carrying it out, the gentlemen said to me, 'That blanket is now where it belongs.'"

The missionaries and Indian agents were so concerned about the ancestral leadership abilities of chiefs over the people that they would hand-pick someone else, someone loyal to them, and name them "Chief," with a given English name. Many First Nations resent the fact that our last names are false names, names given and changed at the residential schools.

However, we confirmed that Baker was not one of these made-up names. It was given by Lt. Joseph Baker to his son,

John Baker. John Baker's mother was Kwasan, the young daughter of Chief Capilano, who greeted Lt. Baker on that hot June day in 1792.

CHAPTER 5

Eslahan Learning Centre, June 2013

*Awakening is about leadership—something to
lead, something to write. It is in the DNA,
the blood.*

CLIFFORD NAEOLE

I put together the pictures I researched on the internet and
any history I could find of written words: what it would
have been like, old calligraphy fonts, and I put red wax
seals on the letters and crest symbols, to make it look more
of the times of the late 1700s. My presentation was staged
to look like an 18th-century writing station. I did it for my
class in the ArrowMight adult program. This program was
started by a Maori elder from New Zealand and it has helped
many aboriginal adult learners who are dyslexic and have a
visual learning style.

When I looked closer at the pictures I had downloaded
from the internet, I noticed that there was a gentleman with

blond hair slouched over a writing tablet in the skiff with Captain Vancouver. Is that him, I thought? With the captain? The naval guard with the musket was looking at the red cedar Salish canoe. In the background, you could see Stanley Park, and smoke raising from the longhouses. There is a native greeting party singing an honour song.

There was strict protocol with any visitors to the shores. First the two chiefs would go out to greet the ships, singing an honour song and circling the ship. Then they would go on board to discuss, with an interpreter, the protocol of the visit. Then trading would commence, and then the captain and an officer or two would go on shore, and the line in the sand would be drawn: the officers would sit on one side and the superior chiefs on the other. Then the protocol of the onshore stays would be discussed.

I brought the panels I had put together into the adult learning classroom at the Eslahan Learning Centre on the designated day.

"Holee—you've gone all out again, Baker!" Candace Halls-Howcroft, one of my teachers, said to me.

"This story has never been told properly, and I want to write it down for everyone to know and learn, which is a big step in our culture," I explained. "They still have doubts about this, even though there are family members with Lt. Joseph Baker's distinctive features—blond hair, light hazel eyes, chubby cheeks and a high, intelligent forehead."

I thought that perhaps the chiefs favoured Joseph Baker because they considered a high forehead to be a status symbol of royalty. They would bind the heads of newborns with cedar planks to create a high, sloped forehead. It was only the noble families that would do this with the babies. The bones were still malleable to be shaped at that young age.

They did not have me give my presentation to the entire class at the ArrowMight program. My teachers asked me to do a private session with just the main teachers. I decided to film the presentation with my digital camera on a tripod. I had my button blanket, my drum and was dressed in all my First Nations' regalia that represented my heritage: Salish paddle skirt (Squamish), the Mary Ebbit chilcat robe (Tlingit) and my cedar bark headdress with ermine, signifying nobility (Kwakiutl).

I brought an inkwell with a feather calligraphy pen, and red wax seals and stamps to represent the old journals. I held my Salish seagoing paddle and used it as a pointer. I spoke about this story. They said they had never seen a presentation that well done, and they presented the DVD to the Maori elder who had started the ArrowMight learning program. He lives in Ottawa. I apparently became a hot topic of conversation as a result of my presentation.

Candace later said to me, "It was the first I heard of it openly. Tell me more. I was like, 'Really!' It opened my eyes and I thought: It is amazing what he is doing. This is something not written—we have only learned it through stories. It was all bottled up inside him, and he was not able to express it due to his previous lack of skill in written communication. It must have been very difficult, and he was now so excited to bring this to the surface."

I became more inspired, and one thing led to another. Mary and I applied twice for a literary grant to the Canada Council for the Arts in Ottawa and were turned down.

Finally, the First Peoples' Cultural Council in Victoria, British Columbia, gave us a grant for archival research. We were very pleased, as we needed that legitimacy to obtain access to the original logbooks and journals of the time, housed in various museums in British Columbia and Hawaii.

CHAPTER 6

BC Archives, Victoria, 2014

*"Do you have permission from the Government of
Britain to do this research?"*

BC ARCHIVES LIBRARIAN

W ade and I looked up, startled, from the microfilm projector where we had just sat down with
the first of two precious cardboard microfilm
boxes labelled B252 and B253. We were beginning to thread
microfilm B252 into the machine when the librarian's loud
voice startled us.

We looked up to see Maureen, the tall, brunette librarian
we had met earlier, towering over us with an imperious look
on her face. She was the same person who had walked us
over to the last of the metal filing cabinets, which contained
the earliest records, and then seated us with a brusque and
impatient manner.

I had wondered why these valuable, early logbook records
were in the cheap grey metal cabinets, as if they were unim-
portant. All the other records seemed to be in beautiful

mahogany custom cabinets. I was also wondering why she was now glaring at us, as if she were ready to escort us out any moment.

In that instant, we realized that her raised voice had caught the attention of the security guard closest to us, who was inside the second entry door, where we had signed in. He looked over at us, concerned. Several researchers at the other scanning machines also looked over at us, wondering what the dissonance was about.

Twenty minutes earlier, we had entered the BC Archives building in Victoria, through beautiful wooden teak carved doors, whose curious symbolism seemed at odds with the rest of the building: water, mountains, sun, a Canada goose and mountain goat, a dogwood flower, Kwakiutl native dancers, a big house and, most curious, a Spanish galleon representing early contact in the coastal waters of British Columbia. I remember thinking briefly, why was Captain Vancouver, or Lt. Joseph Baker, his main mapmaker, missing from the doors?

The first security guard who greeted us was Lance Cooper, friendly and personable. We showed him the email from Judy Thompson at the Maritime Museum of BC, telling us that there were two microfilm records of Lt. Joseph Baker's logbooks at the BC Archives, and the accompanying numbers. A few weeks earlier, I had phoned the archives to find out their opening hours and if there were any restrictions on viewing the material. I was told there were no restrictions, but that we were to be there by 2:00 pm at the latest, as they closed at 4:00 pm.

Lance asked for our driver's licences and proceeded to check on his computer for any prior criminal convictions

(I assumed) or other data. After a few minutes, he handed us back our licences and two small orange cards that read:

Entitles bearer admittance to British Columbia Archives reference room during regular hours. Monday to Friday, 10:00 am to 4:00 pm. Registration no. 14-0469 (M. Tasi) and Registration no. 14-0470 (W. Baker).

Lance also sold us a Royal BC Museum USB device for $10.00, since no other USBs were allowed in the archives. He then took us over to the lockers where he watched carefully as we deposited all our bags, coats, backpacks and water bottles. Lance then escorted us to the second security checkpoint.

Guy Prevost, the guard at the second security checkpoint, eyed us impatiently, realizing that he had to educate us in the protocol of the archives. "What are you bringing in?" he asked, sensing this was our first time in the archives. "You are only allowed a laptop, notebooks, reference papers and the USB. No pens of any kind. Pencils only."

We signed in, with the registration numbers on our entry cards, and walked over to the reference desk, breathing a sigh of relief that we had made it this far. We could feel somehow that we were not entirely welcome, yet not sure why. We had both filled out cards, given to us by Lance, with our names, asking the purpose of our research. Something told me to keep the purpose vague, so we wrote down, "the social history of the early explorers."

I was holding the email from Judy Thompson in the curve of my left arm, prominently displayed on top of my notebook. I quietly thanked Judy in my mind, because it had an official look to it, with the Maritime Museum email heading at the top of the page. Maureen glanced at it as I lowered it so she could read it more clearly, and told her that the museum had informed us that Lt. Joseph Baker's original logbooks were in the archives. She briefly glanced at the email, took our cards stating the purpose of the research, and looked up the microfilm numbers on her computer. She then stood up and walked us over briskly to the cabinets in the far rear corner of the room where the earliest records were kept.

She opened the file drawer, and said with a self-important tone, "Here they are. Do you know how to use the machines?"

"No, this is our first time," I said, looking at the precious microfilm boxes.

I was holding Lt. Joseph Baker's original logbooks; I felt him over two hundred years, suddenly becoming real, like a person airbrushed out of a photograph, slowly being restored.

Maureen gave me an impatient look, and briskly walked us over to another room, with two long banks of scanning machines along two walls. She sat us down at the fourth machine from the door and showed us how to thread the old microfilm, which had been purchased in 1977 from Britain, through the machine.

Then Maureen strode back to her desk.

CHAPTER 7

The Logbooks

I need permission from a fair heart, never from a roaring lion.

SAM KAHAʻI KAAI

W ho is this guy anyway, and are we really connected?" Wade said. "Maybe we'll find out here." The first slide appeared, out of focus, then slowly the machine adjusted the image into view.

"A log of His Majesty's ship *Discovery* from December 22, 1790, to November, 1792, kept by Joseph Baker," I read out loud to Wade. "Purchased from the British government in 1977."

"Third Lieutenant log of his Majesty's ship *Discovery* kept by Lt. Joseph Baker," Wade repeated, mesmerized by the old transcript.

He sat quietly looking at his ancestor's writing. It was like being visited by a seafaring ghost, or watching an old black-and-white movie. The writing was even and to the point, distinguished by long curls in the capital Ts and long

Ss that looked like Ls. So the word that looked like "filth" was actually "fish."

The next slide slid into view.

March 17th *1791* Light breezes and cloudy.

April 12th Light air with the courses.

April 24th Read prayers to ships company.

May 2[d] Punished Blake and Davidson for drunken-ness and neglect of duty.

May 10th Shorten sail for Chatham.

May 20th Set the Royals.

June 1st Trained the people to small arms. Set the Royals.

June 9th Cloudy in Royals.

June 12th Read prayers to ships company.

July 2[d] Fresh breezes, took in the Royals .

October 11th Punished Lewis Jones 24 lashes for neglect of duty.

We were transfixed, as if invited personally onto the ship. We could smell the salt air and hear the rolling waves. We were with a young lieutenant as he wrote his "Remarks of the Day." Wade felt the old ship rising from the ocean, coming to life with all the spirits of the deckhands and officers. They were joyous that we had come to visit them, that we were here because we wanted to tell their whole story. This story was so much more than just longitudes and latitudes and brief survey visits near the shores. They were flesh and blood, these young men, excited about the adventures before them. They had sailed off into the unknown, fearless and open-hearted to what they would find.

"WE REPRESENT BRITAIN here," Maureen said pompously, and abruptly startling us from our research, and bringing us back to the present day. She was standing over us, and willing us to give her our full and worried attention.

Wade told me later that he had thought at the moment, "This is the end of the story. We cannot go further." He said that he was already feeling the shame of being escorted out by the security officers.

We looked at her, stunned. I knew intuitively that this was not the time to say something sarcastic like, "Let me call the Queen."

It was as if the air stood still; we did not know what had upset her. Later, I thought it may have been the words we gave for our reason for research: "social history of the early explorers." There is almost nothing written on this by mainstream historians. The BC history books make it seem as if the explorers arrived to deserted villages, with a couple of random canoes. Reading those books, it seemed the ships came in for a few days, did some surveying, met the Spanish ships and then were gone.

I looked up at Maureen, my heart sinking. Wade was still and quiet next to me, his usual demeanour when distressed, typical of his culture. The thought entered my mind: she must have finally taken the time to read the card stating the purpose of our research and noticed the last name, Baker. Perhaps she had not liked something about our manner. She must have sensed our research was very different from that of the usual scholarly PhDs.

"I am going to check if there are any restrictions," she said, with that senior-administrative tone reserved for principals, store managers and keepers of the keys. Maureen strode off with an officious manner, as if she were hoping to find an excuse to ask us to leave, deliciously anticipating asking the security guard to escort us out.

I calmly said to her as she departed, "Don't shut us down before we even start."

Wade and I sat there, not saying a word to each other. It was an extremely uncomfortable feeling for me, like when the overly dutiful and serious airport customs official wants to examine your carry-on, for no reason other than hoping to find something to embarrass you in front of the huge lineup of travellers.

Wade told me later that he felt numb, because it was ingrained in him that this was information he is not supposed to know; that this was breaking the locks and something not permitted. "I am opening the chest of logbooks, where I am not supposed to be." The air was still, like those stifling hot days with no breeze. It felt as if we should not breathe. Lt. Baker's logbooks were still in the microfilm machine, waiting like a drifting ship. They had likely not been read for at least 30 years—they could wait a bit longer.

Both of us went somewhere quiet, internally, with all the years of meditation helpful in creating a safe space around us and the logbooks, like ships in a harbour, waiting for a breeze.

Maureen finally strode back in, looking a little less triumphant, flicking her hair from her shoulders nervously, her eyes flashing unkindly.

"You can proceed. There are no restrictions," she stated.

CHAPTER 8

Remarks of the Day

Love too, to tack with the natives…
LT. JOSEPH BAKER

I looked at Wade silently. We both realized we had to record this information quickly, before something else happened to shut us down. We scrolled through the very similar Remarks of the Day from March, 1791, wondering if there would be any other comments other than "set the royals," "fresh breezes" or "a dozen lashes" for neglect of duty or insolence to a superior officer.

Then we were rewarded for our persistence, and huge excitement welled up when we finally saw a longer paragraph. Wade found it very difficult to read the old English style of handwriting with flourishes. Perhaps it was my private school, English education in Hampshire that finally paid off: after a few pages, I found I could easily scan and retain the lieutenant's writing, and important phrases jumped out from the scanner as if willing me to record them.

I read to Wade:

A PERSONAL JOURNEY OF DISCOVERY

January 7ᵗʰ, 1792, Otarutie [Tahiti] Cloudy with rain, much surf in the Bay, washed and cleaned the ship, many of the Natives on board, behaving very friendly, bringing fowls, plaintains, breadfruit, coconuts, taro to barter for our commodities. Sent out tents and observatory, sent an officer and four petty officers and 7 marines on shore to guard them, unrigged the top mast… The boat returned with Omarrie (Chief) and we saluted him with guns on coming aboard.

January 16ᵗʰ Saluted Otoo (Chief) with 7 guns and a fireworks display.

March 1ˢᵗ Captain purchased vegetables and a few small ships off the natives. Caulking the quarter deck.

March 2ᵈ, 1792, Sandwich Islands 2 or 3 miles out a great many canoes came off to the ship, bringing cloth, mats, and a variety of curiosities of the country to see, but very few hogs, and vegetables, and the few hogs they bring are very small and at an escorbitant price for them.

March 3ᵈ They brought pigs and vegetables at a more moderate price.

March 6ᵗʰ King Tyanna of this side of the island brought some natives on board with him.

March 7ᵗʰ At 2 Tacked & Love too to tack with the

natives. It was determined to put Towerero, the native
of Morotor ashore here as Tyanna had promised him
a comfortable situation.

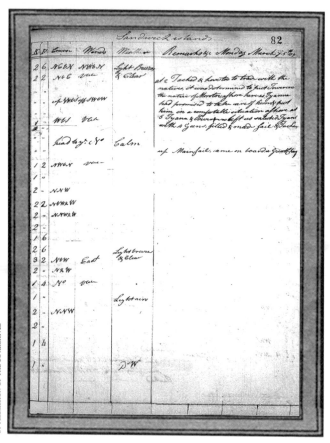

When Wade read this, he felt a connection between himself
and Joseph Baker finally come to life, that feeling of the
excitement of the men and chiefs, racing against each other
for prestige. The Hawaiian canoes were very fast, narrow in

design and could slice through the ocean much faster than the more cumbersome British sloops.

March 7th 1792 At 5 pm, Tyanna and Towerero left us, and we saluted Tyanna with 4 guns, made sail and tacked up the main sail and he then came on board, the Great Chief.

March 27th Fine, pleasant weather. The Captain landed with a guard and the longboat was sent ashore with empty casks and the boats returned to the launch bringing a load of water. Left an officer and a party of marines ashore and they were given two large houses to stay in which were Taboo'd so that none of the natives might come in without their permission. The natives along with two men from the Chatham assisted our people in caulking the Quarter Deck.

March 28th Many of the natives alongside trading… we landed with a party… returned… the natives behaved very friendly… The Chatham anchored in the Big Bay.

March 29th Wychoon Bay At noon saw the Chatham coming around the East point of the Bay, a great number of the natives alongside with great quantities of water, melons, taro, yams, sweet potatoes, and c & c.

I felt that these encampments were where daily socializing occurred, and the learning of each other's cultures.

March 15.ᵗʰ … natives bringing yams in great plenty, sailmakers making… for the masts.

The *Discovery* and the *Chatham* then leave the Sandwich Islands at the end of March, 1792, and set sail for the coast of America.

April 7.ᵗʰ Very smooth water, the surface of the sea covered with a species of Medusa Vanlea, commonly called Portuguese Man of War, saw a bird, flying to the northwest, which I took to be a duck, two or three other birds about the ship.

April 12.ᵗʰ Shortened sail for Chatham, made sail again.

April 19.ᵗʰ Several whales and seals about the ship… land in sight…

April 25.ᵗʰ Found a strong current welling up inshore. Two canoes came off to the ship.

April 27.ᵗʰ Fine black sand.

Then, here in his logbook, Lt. Baker gives detailed land bearings. Followed by more details about activities on and off board the ship.

April 27.ᵗʰ Several canoes about the ship… Punished John Monroe with 2 dozen lashes for insolence to his

superior officer… Two canoes with fish and venison…
Several canoes alongside with salmon.

July 14.th Invited into an Indian Village, brought trifling presents.

Wade feels that this is when Lt. Baker would have met
Kwasan, the daughter of Chief Capilano.

After this point, Lt. Baker states very little in the logbooks,
other than weather observations, and his next lengthy entry
occurs the following spring, when they are back in the Sandwich Islands. He describes at length justice meted out by two
chiefs in regards to the deaths of two Europeans who were
killed on May 11, 1792.

February 21.st, *1793* At noon, light winds, Tamai-
haiha [Kamehameha I] King of the Island, came
on board.

Light airs with small rain, furled sails, got the sleet
anchor over the side and bent the cable… sent a party
on shore with the observatory and astronomical instruments. Captain Vancouver and some of the officers
visited the shore and were received with much friendship and hospitality by the natives. A great number of
canoes alongside with whom a brisk trade was carried
for hogs, vegetables, water and wood.

March 12.th Fresh Breezes, squally air.

March 19.th Light Breezes and Clear.

Captain Vancouver, having made inquiries of the two Principal Chiefs of these islands (Titeree and Tahoo) respecting the deaths of Lieut. Hergest, agent of the *Daedalus*, and Mr. Gooch, astronomer, who were killed at Wiahoo on 11th May, 1792. He was by them informed that three of the murderers had been already put to death, but that there remained three others who should be delivered up on our arrival at Wahoo. One of the chiefs of the Island, named Tamahemeh [King Kamehameha I] now went on board, with orders to that effect. They all agreed that these three were guilty beyond the possibility of a doubt. The condemned prisoners were brought into a canoe alongside

Several canoes about the ship. In a double canoe, the Chief immediately declared them to be the principals concerned in the murder of Sergeant Gooch, and the seaman belonging to the *Daedalus*. It was stated that this person was in the *Daedalus* boat at the time this unhappy transaction took place, and there was evidence that proved the guilty person beyond the possibility of a doubt. The next day, a canoe came alongside and one of their own chiefs shot them to death, by whorling them through the head with a pistol in the presence of the officers and ships company, about 50 of their own canoes being about the ship, though at some distance. Fresh breezes, squally air.

Wade feels this shift back to reporting the weather was his ancestor's way of relieving stress about incidents. Then the ships sail to return to the West Coast of Canada.

April 29ᵗʰ 1793 A number of whales about the ship.

May 3ᵈ The natives are peaceable and friendly.

May 14ᵗʰ Punished Osborne with 12 lashes for quar-relling and fighting. Several canoes alongside, the Natives trading peacefully with their skins of which they appeared to have a great number. Canoes alongside with fish and sea otter skins.

June 1ˢᵗ Three canoes alongside trading for skins

June 3ᵈ Four canoes alongside trading for skins

June 12ᵗʰ Canoes alongside trading for sea otter skins. At noon at an Indian Village. Several canoes about the ship. Sent party ashore to cut wood. Several canoes alongside trading for sea otter skins.

June 16ᵗʰ Several canoes alongside.

CHAPTER 9

BC Archives, Victoria

My parents had broken through the shackles of dogma.

FRANZ BOAS

W ade and I had viewed 200 pages of the logbook when a new researcher sat down on our right. He placed his laptop almost on top of my arm. Annoyed, I moved it over. I then realized that there was probably a reason he was being so irritating. I asked him about his research, and he introduced himself as Grant Barrows, from the University of Texas.

Now that we were being cordial to each other, Grant said with a small smile, "You know, that machine you're using does not work. You can sit there all day, then get home, and find out that nothing has been saved to the USB."

It did not surprise me that Maureen, the reference librarian, had placed us at a defective machine. Adjusting the yarmulke on his head, Grant said, "You can use this machine in a few minutes when I'm finished. They always give the new people that one."

We moved over to the new machine, and rethreaded the microfilm. It was so brittle and old that the first few slides broke off. Maureen came rushing over in an instant; we realized she had positioned herself to be able to watch us through the windows. However, her manner was more pleasant than before. She had seen us chatting with the other researcher, who was obviously a highly regarded regular. With what seemed to be her clearly defined sense of social order, she realized we were now part of the archives' academic research community, and were perhaps worthy of more respect.

"What is happening?" she demanded. We showed her the microfilm, and she commented that it was just the first few blank slides that had broken off. Maureen helped us rethread the microfilm into the machine and moved the tape to page 201.

Our new friend from Texas told us we could stay at the archives until 8:00 pm. "It officially closes at 5:00 pm, but you can keep scanning until 8."

The room became eerily quiet after 5:00 pm. There was only Wade and I, the ever-present security guard and the ghosts in the records, spirits hoping someone would release them and bring their knowledge to the world.

At 6:00 pm, our eyes were tired from the long hours focusing on the small, old English script. We packed up and left. Strolling back to our hotel, the Harbour Towers on Quebec Street, we crossed in front of the Parliament Buildings and walked under the blossoming cherry trees.

Later, we went for an oyster dinner at Pescatore's Fish House and Oyster Bar on Humboldt Street, where we recognized another researcher from the archives.

Alan McGowan, a professor from New York City, joined us for dinner. He was very interested in our work, and said he was researching Franz Boas, who was a pioneer of early work in anthropology and an opponent of scientific racism. Alan also rejected the evolutionary approach to the study of culture and was very appreciative of any Alert Bay contacts we could introduce him to. We were pleased to give him Gloria Webster's information. Gloria is an expert on Kwakiutl culture and history and lives in Alert Bay.

Alan wanted to give George Hunt, a descendant of Robert and Mary Hunt, much more credit for his work in helping Franz Boas at the time. We had a wonderful seafood dinner together; it was exciting to feel we were part of the leading edge of research about the contributions of the indigenous population to the early explorers and the prominent role of oral history.

We had already had our first taste of discovery, finding that mainstream historians had missed something or deliberately chose to rely on later missionary and scholarly interpretations. We remembered the museum guide in Lahaina who told us in 2008 that there was no socializing with the natives and that the ship's officers never left the ship.

We knew from oral history that this was not the case. Now we had written proof, and we had just started the research!

CHAPTER 10

Maritime Museum of BC, Victoria

Set the Royals.

LT. JOSEPH BAKER

The next day we had an appointment at the Maritime Museum of BC at 10:30 am. We walked around the Inner Harbour, past The Empress Hotel's large lawns and gardens, and up Government Street. We were early, so we strolled into Murchie's for some locally made turkey roll pastries, mousse dessert, fruit and the delicious Murchie's coffee, all served on a silver tray. We sat in the peaceful and quiet tearoom at the rear, pleased with the early results of our research.

We arrived at the Maritime Museum and looked at all the books on the gift shop shelves, once again seeing nothing about indigenous navigation. Wade explained that the West Coast natives were master navigators, reading the stars, currents, waves, the taste of the water, observing the sea foam, how and when the winds change, the smell of the water—all this enabled them to travel thousands of miles without charts.

A young lady came into the shop, and told us, "I am here to take you upstairs to the library. Have you ever been in a birdcage elevator? This is the oldest, continually operated one in North America." She slid open the intricately carved metal door, and Wade sat on the small chair. The ancient elevator creaked and moaned, and we slowly rose up, arriving on the third floor a few minutes later.

Judy Thompson was waiting for us. She had a pleasant and engaging demeanour, and we thanked her for the information about the logbooks. We shared our experience at the archives. "Oh yes," she said with a smile. "I've heard they can be like that." We also shared our excitement about the early findings from the microfilm. We found out later that she had worked all over the world, helping various governments with their democratic election processes, and was very knowledgeable about history and politics in general.

She pointed to some books that had been laid out for us. A very large, leather-bound book was on some foam blocks.

"This is the 1798 copy of the published journals of Captain Vancouver, compiled by his brother, John Vancouver," Judy said. "And here are some books that are a record of his voyages, compiled by W. Kaye Lamb and published in 1984."

Wade asked Judy if she knew what "Set the Royals" meant. She said she did not, but would look into it for us. Later she became very interested in our findings, and started doing further research on her own to help us. We were very grateful for her assistance.

Wade started reading through the Lamb book, and I turned my attention to the 1798 journals.

There was an introduction written by Captain Vancouver's brother, John Vancouver.

Captain Vancouver has made many curious observations on the natural history of the several countries he had visited, and on the manners, customs, laws, and religion of the various people with whom he had met, or amongst whom he had occasionally resided; but had been induced to postpone these miscellaneous matters, lest the regular diary of the voyage should be interrupted by the introduction of such desultory observations… These he had intended to present in the form of a supplementary or concluding chapter, but was prevented from doing so, by the unfortunate event of his illness and death… Most of the papers, which contain these interesting particulars, are too concise and too unconnected for me to attempt any arrangement of them… I shall venture to adjoin them to the History of the Voyage…

This seemed curious to us. As we continued our research, we would discover that the story of Captain Vancouver and his mapmaker was developing in an unusual direction; there was more to the story than most people realized.

Judy explained to us that the original journals were likely in the Maritime Museum in Vancouver or in England.

Wade Baker in the Maritime Museum of BC, Victoria, 2014

CHAPTER 11

Vancouver Maritime Museum, 2014

Till my soul is full of longing
for the secret of the sea,
and the heart of the great ocean
sends a thrilling pulse through me.

HENRY WADSWORTH LONGFELLOW

The following week, I presented myself at the Maritime Museum in Vancouver, which has a beautiful setting on the shores of English Bay. Wade had asked me to read the journals for him, as he found the old English writing style almost unreadable because of his dyslexia. We agreed that we would meet each day, after I finished the research, at the Starbucks in North Vancouver, at Third and Lonsdale, and we would go over the summary findings in the journals together.

I parked the car by the museum, and watched the ocean swells washing up on the shore. I saw a small rowboat pulling up onto the sand, and pictured Lt. Baker and his native friends doing the same so many years ago.

Walking into the building, I noticed a sign on the wall for the new art exhibit: DISCRIMINATION MEETS DETERMINATION. This could this be the theme for our book, I thought.

I walked up to the front desk and, now accustomed to museum reception gatekeeping, said, "I have an appointment with Lea Edgar, the head librarian and archivist." The staff asked me to sign in and called downstairs for Lea. While I was waiting for Lea, I wandered over to the historical exhibits and saw a beautiful brass navigational sextant and telescope in a case. The adjacent wording stated that these belonged to Lt. Joseph Baker, and had been loaned by his family to the museum. I later asked the museum if we could contact the family to include them in this story, but was told that the original donor information was no longer available.

When the archivist arrived, I was surprised to see a very intelligent-looking young woman with kind, hazel eyes. After our experience at the BC Archives, I was pleasantly surprised. Lea opened up the rope and led me past the sign saying AUTHORIZED PERSONNEL ONLY, and we walked down a long flight of stairs, past several small offices and antique paintings of ships on the walls.

A poster of Captain Vancouver, dated 2007, showed only his back, gazing out to sea. I later found out that no known confirmed portrait of George Vancouver exists. Apparently, the portrait that was often shown in early history books is not, in fact, Captain Vancouver. The oil painting that is in the National Portrait Gallery collection in England, is "Probably George Vancouver" by "Unknown Artist." (The Canadian commemorative stamp for the 250th anniversary of Captain Vancouver's birth issued on June 22, 2007, is the only stamp ever issued of a prominent person that does not show their face.[6])

This was our second hint that something may be amiss with how history has documented the Captain, the first being that curious introduction to the 1798 journals.

Lea directed me to a large work area, with three leather-bound journals. "You can only use pencils, she said, "and you must use gloves." I was prepared, as I had brought along the white cotton gloves that Chi Pilialoha, the docent at the old Lahaina High School print museum, had given me in Maui.

I was very excited. "Are these the original Vancouver journals?" I asked.

Lea looked at me with an air of mystery. "When you first called, I checked our list of high-value books in the vault. If we had the original, I knew it would be worth at least a million dollars, and it may be restricted. I did not realize his original journals have disappeared! No one has requested to look at his journals for a very long time, as far as I know."

I was intrigued, as I knew that several more books had been written in the last couple of years about the early explorers and their early mapping of the coast.

There was a young researcher sitting at the table, and Lea introduced me to her, "This is Sarah Emily Mackenzie. She is a PhD student, researching the early explorers as well. She may often be here at the same time as you are. Let me know if you need anything. However, I am quite busy with work today." Lea went back to her office, leaving me with the journals.

I started to chat to Sarah, and I told her my husband and I were looking for information or notes about the explorers' interactions with the local natives, as there was little or no information about the social history in the mainstream texts.

Sarah told me that Captain Vancouver's journals had likely been edited, and she shared her experience as a PhD history student. She told me that if I noticed the writing style was very different from one section to another, I could infer that that section had been edited. She shared that, at university, they were trained using the Bible to learn and interpret where passages had been rewritten, edited and deleted. Sarah encouraged me to view everything through a critical lens, as stories may have been circulated in England to project a certain slant or perspective on Captain Vancouver's explorations.

It was a pleasure to have some company, and I enjoyed our brief, hushed conversational interludes between the painstaking reading of the old English journals. Particularly challenging was the fact that S was written with what looked like an F. For example, what looked like "diftnct" was in fact "distinct." Or what looked like "veffel" was actually "vessel." I found I could only read for about 30 minutes before my eyes would become sore, and my hand would cramp up from writing in pencil. I later discovered that typing on my iPad was easier on my hands.

Sarah understood our purpose of looking for an indigenous perspective on the voyages of the early European explorers.

"Well, we are on traditional Coast Salish land here," she said kindly.

CHAPTER 12

First Journal of Captain Vancouver

A pleasing and courteous deportment distinguished these people.

CAPTAIN VANCOUVER ON THE COAST SALISH PEOPLE,

APRIL 1792

A *voyage of discovery to the North Pacific Ocean and around the world. in which the Coast of North West America has been carefully examined and accurately surveyed. Undertaken by His Majesty's command principally with a view to ascertain the existence of any navigable communication between the North Pacific and North Atlantic Oceans And performed in the years 1790, 1791, 1792, 1793,1 794, & 1795 In the Discovery Sloop of War, and Armed Tender Chatham Under the Command of Captain George Vancouver*

In three volumes, printed for G. G. and J. Robinson, and J. Edwards, Paternoster-Row,London, Pall Mall, 1798.

I put on my white cotton gloves, opened my notebook and pulled out a pencil from the pencil holder. Very gently, I opened the leather-bound, first volume of the journals.

I anticipated I would be looking for the proverbial needle in a haystack to find references to the native people, judging from how little was in the mainstream school texts and recent publications about the voyages.

The first pages listed the officers on board:

Discovery
> George Vancouver
> Zachariah Mudge
> Peter Puget
> Joseph Baker
> Joseph Whidbey

Chatham
> Lieutenant W.R. Broughton
> James Hanson
> James Johnstone

As I scanned the pages, I found many many entries about the local chiefs, kings and native translators aboard the ships. I was now with Captain Vancouver, walking with him in Tahiti and the Sandwich Islands (Hawaii).

January, *1792* I had the mortification of finding on inquiry that most of the friends I had left here in the year 1777, both male and female, were dead. Ottoo, with his father, brothers and sisters, Potatao, and his family, were the only chiefs of my old acquaintance that were now living.

Mr. Broughton had prepared a present in so

handsome a way that I considered it a sufficient compliment to the young king from us both.

As soon as the ship was secured, Mr. Whidbey and myself, attended by Mr. Broughton, with intention to fix on an eligible spot for our tents, and for transacting our necessary business on shore, and afterward to pay our respects to his Otaheitean Majesty.

A small boat for the Chatham was to be built, and a great repair was necessary to her large cutter.

The portrait of Captain Cook, drawn by Mr. Webber in 1777, is always deposited in the house of the ruling Chief of Matavai, and is become the public register. Chief Poeno was the current Chief of Matavai.

We were in Karakakooa Bay, where Captain Cook fell... yet to us it had produced an asylum, where the hospitable reception, and friendly treatment of such could not be surpassed by the most enlightened nation on earth.

WADE AND I later spoke to Richard Mickelsen, Director of the Story of Hawaii Museum at the Queen Ka'ahumanu Centre in Kahalui, Maui. He was excited to share his fascinating and extensive knowledge of Captain Cook. Richard (Buck) was an enthusiastic and crusty old seaman with piercing blue eyes and a silver beard, descended from Norse mariners.

Richard told us that the Pacific Islanders had an elite fraternity of navigators, taught from childhood to read nautical information.

Wade added that his ancestors could also read over 30

different meanings from the moon's shapes and celestial movements.

Richard continued: "The islander's canoes could stream forward at 12 to 14 knots and travelled over 15 million miles. European ships at the time could only go at four knots because they were round in shape.

"Captain Cook arrived in 1778 at the exact time of the God Lono, the god of nature, harvest and fertility. This was the rainy season, the season of Lono, October or November, and the kona storms were coming in. He stayed three months in the Hawaiian Islands, and was treated like a god. The prophecies said that Lono would arrive on floating islands, and would have incredible wealth. This suited the priests or Kahunas as well, as it proved their prophecies. The people gave Captain Cook all the harvest and resources. When he decided to leave, a short way out from shore in February, 1779, the foremast broke on the HMS *Resolution*. He made the unfortunate decision to return to Kealakekua Bay. It was protected, and the only safe place for landing to make repairs. The foremast was crucial to sailing. However, the time of Lono was now over, and the God Ku (the god of man and his deeds) was now in power.

"A famine had been created, and there were rising tensions that escalated over a few days. The officers dismantled the fencing around the Heiau (sacred temple) on the beach, and there were accusations about a missing cutter. A council of war was held on the ship, and a plan was made to take Chief Kalaniopu'u, the uncle of the future King Kamehameha I. Guard boats were sent in to hold the bay.

"Cook grabbed one arm of the ruling chief, and the chief's

wife grabbed the other arm. Cook was used to grabbing the ruling chief and taking him hostage. This had worked for him on all the other islands. He did not realize he was not allowed to touch royalty here. As the two of them tussled over the chief, things became very tense, and Cook realized he had to leave quickly. A warrior put his club between Cook and the Chief, and separated the two. There were now warriors surrounding Captain Cook, and one warrior clubbed him. When he groaned, they realized he was not a god, and he was killed. Muskets were now firing from the guard boats in the direction of the beach, 65 yards off shore, out of spear range. The muskets were not accurate, and shooting went in all directions. Cannons were fired from the ship."

According to Uncle Sam, many members of the Royal family perished that day as well; the future King Kamehameha was also wounded, however not fatally.

I imagined the scene in that moment.

SEVENTY-NINE MEN LAY dead and dying on the beach. The shoreline ran red with blood. Everyone went silent. No one moved, appalled at what had just happened. The birds had stopped singing. The only sound was the ancient murmuring of the waves. By this time, Captain Charles Clerke and Vancouver, who at the time was a young midshipman, had just arrived on the beach.

IN AUGUST 2015, I spoke to elder Joyce Gillcoat in Maui, and told her I felt there was something missing in all the stories about this incident.

"What do you think happened next? " I asked her.

Joyce lit a candle, and pondered. "Hoʻoponopono [ancient healing and forgiveness ceremony] must have happened," she said quietly. "There must have been Hoʻoponopono, because otherwise they would not have cremated him. They realized Captain Cook was not a god, but a mortal of high stature."

I spoke to another elder in Lahaina that same day who confirmed that Hoʻoponopono would have had to happen, to cleanse the area of the negative energy and return it to a sacred place of peace.

Wade felt that Captain Charles Clerke and the 21-year-old Vancouver must have sat down together with the future King Kamehameha and discussed the protocol of what should happen after Hoʻoponopono.

Uncle Sam confirmed that they very likely would have discussed protocol together. They may have all agreed to have his body cremated in the traditional way, to lay in state as a high chief, and to allow some of his remains to return to the ship, and some to be buried in Kealakekua Bay. This was considered the caring way. They knew they had to pacify the situation and make friends with the natives, otherwise the crew of every ship coming in the future would be massacred. There would have also been great concern for the safety of all the men aboard the HMS *Resolution*. This incident affected Vancouver in a profound way, and helped form his character.

RICHARD DESCRIBED FOR us the journeys Cook's midshipman, George Vancouver, subsequently took when he was in command of the *Discovery* (and, incidentally, explained what the "Royals" were). "Vancouver left England in April, 1791, and sailed into the South Atlantic. He would then go around the Cape of Good Hope, and stop at Cape Town, as he could repair the ship, and take on crew and supplies there. Then he headed to Australia (New Holland) via Amsterdam and St. Paul islands (Indian Ocean). Then onto New Zealand. He would then break out into the Pacific Ocean. He would set the Royals, which were good weather sails. They were taken down in bad weather as there would be too much strain on the masts. Then on to Tahiti for the next rest stop. It was not under French control yet. They would pick up firewood, water, supplies and two native interpreters/master navigators. In early 1792, he continued on to the Sandwich Islands (Hawaii). Then onto Monterrey (San Francisco) and up the coast to the now Seattle area, and the Vancouver area. He went up through Georgia Strait, and then around Vancouver Island. Then onto Nootka Sound, and then back to Hawaii. (1793). In 1793 and 1794, he sailed on different routes. His return journey in 1795 took him around Cape Horn and then back to England through the Atlantic Ocean."

I TURNED MY attention back to the journal, and kept scanning for the captain's descriptions of the local social interactions.

January, 1792 A large party of royalty and chiefs hon oured us with their company at dinner, which failed to be a pleasant circumstance solely in consequence of the

138   A VOYAGE OF DISCOVERY

1792.
January.

The queen-mother, although deſtitute of any pretenſions to beauty, and having in her perſon a very maſculine appearance, has yet, in her general deportment, ſomething exceſſively pleaſing and engaging; far from any auſterity or pride, ſhe is endued with a comparative elegance of manners, which plainly beſpeaks her deſcent, and the high ſituation in which ſhe is placed. Although her figure exhibited no external charms of feminine ſoftneſs, yet great complacency and gentleneſs were always conſpicuous; indicating, in the moſt unequivocal manner, a mind poſſeſſing, and alone actuated by thoſe amiable qualities which moſt adorn the human race. All her actions ſeemed directed to thoſe around her with an unalterable evenneſs of temper, and to be guided by a pure diſintereſted benevolence. Self, which on moſt occaſions is the governing principle in the conduct of theſe iſlanders, with her was totally diſregarded; and indeed, ſuch was her very amiable diſpoſition, that it counterbalanced any diſadvantages ſhe might labour under in a deficiency of perſonal attractions.

The portrait of *Fierre te* on canvas would moſt probably be generally thought intitled to a preference; yet ſhe appeared by no means to poſſeſs either mental endowments, or other excellent qualities, in the ſame degree with the queen-mother; if ſhe had them, they were latent, and required ſome particular exertion to bring them into action. Her ſoftneſs and effeminacy afforded her ſome advantage over her ſiſter; yet there was a ſhyneſs, want of confidence and manner in her general demeanor, that evinced her motives to be leſs diſintereſted. We were however led to believe, that ſhe was not deſtitute of the amiable qualities, though to us they did not appear ſo conſpicuous as in the character of the queen-mother. Of the two ladies, *Fierre te* was by far the favorite of *Pomurrey*, at leaſt we had every reaſon to think ſo by the general tenor of his conduct. Notwithſtanding this preference, he was obſerved in ſeveral inſtances to abide implicitly by the advice and opinion of the queen-mother, and to treat her with great affection and the moſt...

weather being extremely hot, and the cabin excessively crowded… On this occasion the wives of Pomurrey and the wife of Mahav were permitted to sit with us at the table and partake of the repast.

Some of the royal females had now joined our party, and as Pomurrey had not yet paid Mr. Broughton a visit, we all went on Board the *Chatham*.

In the evening, we were very fortunate in our display

of fireworks, I instructed Chief Pomurrey's youngest wife. With a little of my assistance, she fired several rockets, a Cathanne wheel, some flower pots, and balloons. The young king, with his brothers and sister, honoured the encampment also with their presence. Understanding that our royal party were about to leave us for some days, presents were made them on the occasion with which, highly delighted with their excursion, and the reception by us, they departed.

Fierrete, the Queen Mother, King Pomurrey's wife … has in her general deportment, something excessively pleasing and engaging. Free from any austerity or pride, she is endued with a comparative elegance of manners, which plainly bespeaks her descent, and the high fixation in which she is placed. Although her figure exhibited no external charms of feminine softness, yet great complacency and gentleness were always conspicuous, indicating in the most unequivocal manner, a mind possessing, and alone actuated, by those amiable qualities which most adorn the human race. All her actions seemed directed to those around her with an unalterable evenness of temper, and to be guided by a pure disinterested benevolence… The islanders had a very amiable disposition towards the Queen Mother…

Lea came over to where I was reading the journals, and said, "Mary, in the references, it says that the original journals have disappeared, including the drafts he sent to the Admiralty. They have disappeared as well. There is a mystery here!" She went back to her office to continue her work for the museum.

Sarah was listening to the conversation at the end of the table, and looked at me curiously.

"What should I do," I asked. "This project is getting bigger and more mysterious every day."

"There is a apparently a story about the nephew of the prime minister at the time who was sent on the ship. This was common in the day, and Captain Vancouver sent him back, as he was so much trouble," said Sarah. "This nephew spread nasty rumours, apparently. Mary, you just ride the wave and see where it goes."

I continued with my reading, hoping I would find something about this nephew of the prime minister in the captain's journals. I continued to record the Captain's words exactly as I read them, as his writing was extremely descriptive.

January, *1792* I cannot avoid acknowledging how great was the disappointment experienced in consequence of the earlier impressions I had of the natives superior personal endowments. They themselves freely admit the alteration, which in a few years has taken place and seem to attribute much to the lamentable diseases introduced by European visitors, to which many of their finest women, at an early period of life, have fallen sacrifice.

.... for a large proportion of the crew belonging to the *Bounty* should have become so infatuated as to sacrifice their country, their honour, and their lives, to the female attachments at Otaheite [Tahiti]. The objects of their particular regard, by whom they have children, we frequently saw.

On March 18, 1792, Captain Vancouver and his ships left
the Sandwich Islands for the Canadian west coast.

April, 1792 Soon after we anchored, a canoe was seen
paddling towards the ship with the greatest confidence,
and without any sort of invitation, came immediately
alongside. During the afternoon, two others visited the
Discovery, and some repaired to the *Chatham*, from different parts of the Coast in sight, by which it appeared
that the inhabitants who are settled along the shores of
this country may probably have their residence in…

A pleasing and courteous deportment distinguished
these people. Their countenance indicates nothing
ferocious. Their hair is long, black, clean and neatly
combed, generally tied in a club behind, although some
amongst them had their hair in a club in front also.
Their features partook rather of the European character;
their colour a light olive. their stature was under the
middle size, none exceeding five feet, six inches. They
were tolerably well limbed, though slender in their
persons. And bore little or no resemblance to the people
of Nootka, nor did they have the least knowledge of
that language… dressed in garments that nearly covered them, made of deer, bear, fox and river otter, one
or two sea otter skins were observed. They seemed to
prefer the comforts of cleanliness to the paintings of
their bodies. Their canoes, calculated to carry about
8 people, wrought out of a single tree, resembled a
butchers tray.

The dogs belonging to this tribe resembled those of

Pomerania. They were all shorn as close to the skin as sheep in England, and so compact were their fleeces, that large portions could be lifted up by a corner... it was very fine long hair, capable of being spun into yarn. This gave me reason to believe that their woollen clothing may be comprised in part of this material, mixed with a finer wool. Their garments were very fine and extremely well wrought."

Johnstone's Straits. From a sketch by J. Sykes, 1793

When I read this to Wade at the end of the day, both of us sipping on a latte at Starbucks, he said, "Those are Coast Salish people for sure!"

We have a picture of our daughter modelling a beautiful white dress, created by Wade's sister Pam (Himikalas) Baker. Pam had placed furs on Sierra's shoulders and I believe my sister-in-law must have sensed this subconsciously from her ancestry, as most current history books at the time only talked about cedar bark clothing. Cedar bark clothing would only have been worn in very hot weather during the short, summer months. Otherwise, it would have been raining and cool, and furs would have been the natural choice.

April, 1792 In this traffic of trading for iron and beads, they were scrupulously honest, particularly in fixing their bargain with the first bidder... They did not entertain the least idea of accepting presents, for on my giving them some beads, medals, and iron, they instantly offered furs on return, and seemed much distressed when declined.

The following day, I came back to go through the second journal. There was a very strong smell of dust in the museum and the staff members were sneezing. I was startled to see a life-sized mannequin of an RCMP officer placed immediately to the left of where I had been sitting. Sarah, the PhD researcher, was there, too. Pleased to see me, she explained, "Oh, they are restoring his outfit."

Is that a sign that there are forces that do not want this information made public, I thought, or are the ghosts playing with us?

I met Wade at Starbucks at the end of the day, and could hardly contain my excitement about all the journal entries about the local natives I had been reading.

Wade said, "I realize that what I heard as stories growing up were all true, about the extensive socializing that had occurred. We had to hear the original words of Captain

Vancouver to validate the stories. The government had changed the stories to make it seem as if these were empty lands, waiting to be colonized, just as Walter Joseph had told me. I need to talk to him some more."

I realized we had to go back, once again, to First Nations' oral history and the story of Wade's family to fill in the gaps.

CHAPTER 13

Baker Clan History

*Go and greet the whales, they are coming to
say goodbye.*

MARY CAPILANO, PRINCESS OF PEACE

One of my great-great-grandparents was Chief Joseph Capilano, who was a leading campaigner for First Nations' rights. In 1906, he went to England to meet with King Edward VII to discuss settling land claims in British Columbia. Chief Joseph's mother was Mary Agnes Capilano.

My great-great-great-grandmother held the title "Princess of Peace." I don't know when she was born, but I was told it was sometime around 1840. She was the daughter of a Squamish chief's son and a Yaculta chief's daughter. Those two tribes were Coast tribes, who had been fighting for many years. When Mary Agnes's parents married, now there were blood ties between the tribes, and peace.

My uncle, Chief Simon Baker, told the family history in his autobiography, *Khot-La-Cha*. His grandmother, the wife of Chief Joseph Capilano (also called Mary Agnes), told Simon the story of his maternal ancestors.

She said her grandfather, Chief Payt -Sa-mahk, and his brother Chief George Capilano wanted to make peace with the Yacultas to make their territory safe for their people. Her grandfather took one hundred war canoes, each with 20 men, to where the Yacultas lived to ask for peace to stop the many years of fighting. They spent two days trying to get the Yacultas to believe they really wanted peace. Finally, her grandfather ordered all the men to throw their spears into the water and to empty their muskets by firing them into the water. That's when the Yacultas believed that the Squamish were there in peace, so they got rid of their weapons, too.

My grandmother always said she was a member of the whale family. She would go out in the inlet fishing every day to talk to the whales, as they travelled north. The day she died, she said to her daughter in Squamish, 'Go and greet them, they are coming to say goodbye.' Her daughter ran down to the beach, and saw a whole school of whales coming right into the harbour. When she ran back to tell her mother, she was gone. [7]

My great-great-grandfather was called John Baker. He was from England, and had come here on one of the sailing ships. He met a beautiful Squamish woman, Mary Tsi-yaliya, and they got married. Grannie Lizzie was their daughter. She said her mother had light skin and looked like she had white blood. John Baker had money and he built a hotel in Gastown. Then the hotel burned down and all the money was gone. After he died, Grannie Lizzie and her three sisters, along with her mother, moved back to the Mission reserve.

Chief Simon Baker, in his autobiography, explained, When my grandfather died, they were living on Deadman's Island, the little island where the navy is near Stanley Park. He was buried there. After he died, the Indian people invited my grandmother, Mary Tsiyaliya Baker, to return to the Mission reserve. They had already built the Catholic church. When they brought them over, they had to join the church. my grandmother and her teenaged daughters were told they all had to marry Indians from around there.

Those days, the church did not want to have a half breed marrying a half breed, so they all married Indians from the reserve. My grandmother married Squamish Jacob. The oldest girl, Lizzie, married Chief Joseph, who was the chief of the Mission Reserve.[8]

We had to connect the missing pieces, and I felt that the missing piece was here. That John Baker's grandfather was Joseph Baker. Perhaps the grandson of Captain Vancouver's mapmaker returned to the land his grandfather had charted at the end of the 18th century.

Many First Nations did not want to admit to European ancestry as they were worried about potentially losing Band status, and being excluded from the community. It was another way the Indian Act would ensure the native communities stayed isolated within themselves. I recall one Squamish Chief saying to us in 2008, "I don't want to think about that English guy in my ancestry."

However, Mary and I have learned that it is important

to accept and acknowledge all our ancestry, otherwise parts of us stay invisible that could potentially serve us and the community.

At the beginning of January, 2015, Mary and I spoke to my mother, Emily, and my brother, Frank James Baker, at 80's Restaurant in North Vancouver to update them about the book.

"I was told that John Baker did go back to England to visit, but on his return never spoke about what happened," my mother said.

Copy of an original map drawing by Lt. Joseph Baker of Point Grey/Howe Sound, 1792

Frank said that he knew the names of the two chiefs whom Captain Vancouver met, and that he would let me see the information in a book that he had at home. He later told me that they were Te Khap-a-la nogh and Te Khats-a-lanogh.

It is very unusual that these two chiefs are not mentioned in Captain Vancouver's journals, other than when he writes about meeting two superior chiefs. All throughout Tahiti and Hawaii, he writes detailed descriptions of the names, clothing and social interactions. Therefore, it can be inferred that in this area, his writing has been severely edited.

As I was growing up, I had been told that Lt. Joseph Baker had had three children with the daughter of Chief Capilano, who were known as the Bakers. He then had three more children with her sister or half-sister, after his first wife died. They were the Josephs.

At the beginning of our research, this was all we knew. The reluctance of many in my community to discuss the past, especially the intermarriage and relationships between the early Europeans and the First Nations, presented a challenge. But since Lt. Joseph Baker's tour of duty on board the *Discovery* lasted almost six years, spending summers in what is now the Vancouver area, and winters in Hawaii, we realized we needed to research further in Hawaii.

The Maui elders could possibly know more and their oral history could reveal more about the social interactions between the indigenous people and Captain Vancouver and his crew. What we had learned there in 2013 shed valuable light on what we were discovering now. And we would return again at the end of 2014.

CHAPTER 14

Maui, December, 2013

*Io is the moon and the sun, the stars, the air and
the wind. Io is the ancient murmuring that speaks
before the storm will engulf you.*

SAM KAHAʻI KAAI

W ade and I both felt that we also needed to speak
with Hawaiian elders, to learn their oral history
about the early explorers. Captain Vancouver
had spent more time there than in British Columbia, and
we had seen Joseph Baker's maps in the Lahaina Printsellers.
When Wade and I first started asking about Lt. Joseph Baker
in Maui in 2008, there seemed to be far more interest and
excitement there than in Vancouver.

I emailed the head curator at the Lahaina Restoration
Society in November, 2013, and asked for a meeting on the
first Monday I would be there. She agreed to see me at 10:00
am on December 15.

On the day, I arrived early in Lahaina and found parking
behind the library, close to the shoreline. I walked over to a

small plaque mounted on bricks in the ground. It said, THE BRICK PALACE OF KING KAMEHAMEHA I, and told how it had been built at the command of the king in 1798 and was the first western-style building in the islands. An English convict from Australia fired the the bricks used for the palace.

I thought that the wording on the plaque was faintly condescending, and the tone was different than at other sites, like the Baldwin House or the Old Lahaina Court and Custom House museum. Another plaque pointed the way to the healing rock, visible at low tide.

I was getting my familiar feeling of irritation and frustration, so decided to go into the small cafe I noticed tucked into a side street, hidden behind hanging vines and flowers. It looked like a locals' hangout. At the Sunrise Cafe, I ordered a fruit salad and a coffee, and sat relishing the warm tropical breeze, listening to the locals' conversation about surfing and nightlife.

After my snack, I walked around the back of the Baldwin House and up the stairs, following the sign to the administration office. It was unusually cool for Maui, and I was glad I had brought a thin shawl. I had my Australian hat on; I thought it gave me a roaming-anthropologist look that might put the historical society people at ease. A pleasant young Hawaiian girl was sitting at reception. I told her I had an appointment with the head curator.

Victoria came out of her office to greet me. She had a missionary look about her, a rather serious, firm and closed manner. I felt some tension, as if perhaps she did not have time for an outsider trying to dig up old stories from the 1700s that did not fit any boxes. I maintained a cheery tone, and told her I had just visited the King Kamehameha brick palace site. I must not have sounded suitably impressed, as she replied, "Yes, that site needs some restoration work, and perhaps the plaque needs rewording. We just don't have the budget right now."

"Do you have any books or records on the early explorers and the history around them?" I asked.

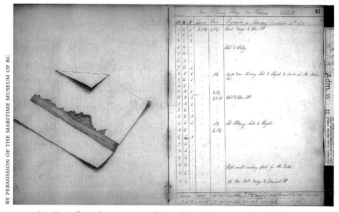

Lt. Joseph Baker: original sketch and "Remarks of the Day"

"No," she said, "but I recommend you go to the Lahaina Luna High School. There is a print museum there. The records are not well kept and we don't have a list of items, but you are welcome to look around there. Chi is working there today. She may be able to help you. I do know that this Lt. Joseph Baker was an artist. I have seen his drawings, called the Baker drawings. But, I don't know where they are now."

I had a sinking feeling that I would be spending the next week looking through piles of unorganized documents.

"Do you know any elders that I could speak to?" I asked.

She gave me a firm look. "Yes, but they may not wish to talk to you."

"Well," I said, noticing her large boardroom table covered with books. "May I sit here and work on my notes for awhile?"

CHAPTER 15

The Maui Cultural Elders

Once you release your words, you cannot take them back. It is a contract between you and the Creator.

SAM KAHA'I KAAI

A t that very moment, her cell phone rang. She answered it and said, "Hi, Auntie Patty," and started a lengthy conversation. Listening, I soon realized that Auntie Patty Nishiyama must be one of the local elders. I sat at the table patiently for ten minutes, and then wrote on a piece of paper, "May I speak to her?"

"Auntie Patty, I have a writer from Canada here. Do you want to talk to her?" she said. I reached out my hand, and she gave me the phone. I knew I had ten seconds to make a good impression. The voice on the other end of the line had that beautiful, melodious Hawaiian accent that is so full of aloha—it can melt away all the background chatter from years of anxiety and criticism. I told Auntie Patty I would like to speak to her, or anyone else she knew, about the early explorers. I told her my husband was Native Canadian, and

A PERSONAL JOURNEY OF DISCOVERY

that I had been 20 years in his community. I explained that I understood about respect and protocol.

"Can I take you for lunch?" I asked.

Patty answered, "I do know someone, but I don't know if he will talk to you. Let me call you back."

I handed the phone back to Victoria, who was reaching for her cell. Then I realized I had not given Auntie Patty my phone number. "She will call me back," I said. Victoria left her phone on the edge of the boardroom table, and went to another room. Five minutes later, the phone rang, and I picked it up, hoping I would know how to answer the call. It was Auntie Patty.

"Uncle Sam will speak to you, and here is his phone number," she said.

"Thank you so much! Can I take you out for lunch?" I replied.

"No, it is okay. Just talk to Uncle Sam. Take him out for lunch," Patty said, a smile in her voice.

Victoria came in, and I gave her the cell phone back graciously, thanking her for her assistance; I was very grateful that she had connected me with a local elder.

I drove immediately back to Maui West Gardens in West Maui, and rushed up the two flights of stairs to the unit where I was staying, past the bougainvillea and pikake flowers, roosters and palm trees. I almost collided with the maid's cart on the landing. I laid out the map of Maui next to the phone, opened up my notebook and made sure two pens were nearby. Then I picked up the phone and dialled Uncle Sam. I told him Auntie Patty had given me his number, and that I was trying to find out about the early explorers, as there was little published information in Vancouver about their relationships with the local natives. I explained I had only found a quote or two about natives in canoes coming out to meet the ships.

Sam Kahaʻi Kaai (Uncle Sam) answered with a curt, no-nonsense tone and a strong Hawaiian accent, "Why do you care about it?"

I explained that oral history said my husband was descended from Lt. Joseph Baker, the mapmaker on Captain Vancouver's ship, and that there was nothing in the mainstream history books about this.

"I am researching the early explorers during the period from 1791 to 1810. There is very little written in the social history texts about this time, just the technical aspects of the mapmaking and exploration," I said.

Uncle Sam then proceeded to talk and scold me for three hours. I wrote as fast as I could, amazed at what he knew. Later he would tell Wade and me, amused at the memory, "I told Auntie Patty when she called me and said I should talk to you, 'Why should I have an opinion about these matters? I'm not running for office.'"

CHAPTER 16

Kings and Captains

Everyone is fighting for the ear of the Lonely One,
the King: King Kamehameha I.

SAM KAHAʻI KAAI

S am Kahaʻi Kaai started talking about Captain Cook. He said that Captain Cook's method was to grab the highest chief on shore, and hold him until everything settled down. This did not work in Hawaii, where the only sport was military training and action. When he grabbed the chief in Kealakekua Bay, several members of the royal family rushed in. According to Uncle Sam, 75 chiefs of the royal Hawaiian family were also killed on the beach that day, along with three British officers.

"The winner writes the story from the winner's point of view," said Sam. "Captain Vancouver and King Kamehameha I met when Captain Cook visited the Islands, and Vancouver was a young midshipman aboard the *Resolution*, during Captain Cook's last great voyage of exploration. When Captain Vancouver first met King Kamehameha, they were both young and not at the high status they were at later years, however they were considered equals.

"Later, Captain Vancouver and his men came to Hawaii in the winter, then went back up the northwest coast of America in the summer. They went back and forth like that for three years. They were the first snowbirds. The *Discovery* first landed on the island of Maui in Maalaea Bay, just west of the present day Kihei, as it was considered safe anchor. The two sides were in awe of each other, and they would have had a royal welcome from King Kamehameha when they returned each winter. Captain Vancouver did not do King Kamehameha any ill. He was highly respected, and a great friend and confidante.

"King Kamehameha was only chief of the Big Island of Hawaii when they met. He had brought 400 years of fighting to an end. He was called the great unifier. By 1795, King Kamehameha had conquered Maui, Lanai, Kahoolave and Molokai and acquired control of Oahu at the Battle of Nu'uanu. Kauai and Nihau, under the leadership of Kaumuali'i, submitted to King Kamehameha's rule in 1810.

"Captain Vancouver negotiated with Great Britain that King Kamehameha and Britain would protect the Big Island from American or other interests. The treaty was never ratified, but King Kamehameha flew the British flag up until the war of 1812 between Britain and the US. At the end of the war, out of respect to Captain Vancouver, the Hawaiian flag was a hybrid of the British flag and the US showing the eight Hawaiian islands as eight stripes.

"The word 'own' did not exist in our dictionary. We thought we were sharing the land."

I asked Uncle Sam about how the locals had been stereotyped.

"Every morning, the natives would visit the ship. Some swam out, and the bark cloth would melt in the waves. The officers created a temporary camp on the beach, and would wear just their loose shirts. no silk stockings, they removed them."

King of Hawaii bringing gifts. John Weber, 1784

Sam told me that the Hawaiian sailing vessels were faster than the British ships. Wade and I would later confirm this, when we found Lt. Joseph Baker's logbook entry in which he wrote that he loved "too to tack with the natives."

"Captain Vancouver said: I am going to bring out a cow and a goat. He took so long bringing the cow that the goat came out first. So, the name for a goat in Hawaiian means cow. Captain Vancouver brought gifts to establish resources on the islands so that future ships could collect bounty. Did he bring influenza? Possibly.

"Your ancestor Joseph Baker was the first European to hike up the mountains to Haleakala. The last time Haleakala [East Maui volcano] erupted was when Captain Vancouver was there. It is the place where the sun was released by the demi-god Maui."

WADE SAID, "ORAL tradition says that Chief George Capilano took Captain Vancouver's first name to honour him, as a friend to the Salish people. That is how we kept our history alive, we would take names after great men who were a part of our lives. He was a great man, so carry on his story.

"I remember my Dad and Uncle Bill and the others used to sing this song, 'The Snowbirds,' in the Salish language. That means they would have travelled between the two areas. So, the two peoples knew each other. It is just the rhythm of the sound waves. It is a drumming and singing of the sounds of the universe that comes from the air and the waves."

CHAPTER 17

Kāne Makua

*We thought we were sharing the fruits, not giving
away the soil and the roots.*

SAM KAHAʻI KAAI

After several hours listening to Uncle Sam on the phone, I asked, "Could I meet you tomorrow and buy you lunch?" I knew that this was the protocol for sharing information.

"You can come to my house," he said. I looked at the map and realized that Pukalani was a two-hour drive, and I was still suffering with a sore back from stress and overload in Vancouver.

"Can we meet halfway?" I suggested.

"Where is that?" he said. "I have an acupuncture appointment at 1:00 pm, and needed time to get back for that."

Looking at the map, I saw that the Maui Ocean Center in Maalaea was about halfway for both of us. We agreed to meet at 9:30 am the next day. "Take your vitamins!" Uncle Sam said, with a mischievous tone. "I drive a Toyota silver truck."

I arrived early at the centre, as I was worried there may not be a place to eat open at that time. I was right. I looked around the deserted mall with a sinking feeling. There was one take-out coffee shop where we would have to sit outside on the whale-shaped outdoor bench. Knowing from experience that respected elders were used to be taking care of, I went into the Ocean Center to see when the coffee shop would be open. I explained to the young lady at the reception desk, "I am meeting an elder and want a nice place to be able to talk." She looked at me, confused. This did not fit her usual scenario of frantic-tourist-with-kids-in-tow.

I saw the silver truck drive into the parking lot, and an elderly man with a powerful build slowly got out, leaning on a carved cane. I walked up to him and shook his hand. "I am very honoured you have made the effort to come and meet with me," I said to him warmly.

Sam Kahaʻi Kaai is a Hawaiian cultural elder. He had a strong, wise and mischievous demeanour. He was wearing a carved, whale-bone pendant necklace and had several geometric tattoos on his wrists. They reminded me of the unique triangles also prominent in Coast Salish art. Uncle Sam told me he was from the Makarik ancestral line, from the leaping place of the seven-eyed dragon.

We started to walk towards the Ocean Center entrance, and I said, worried, "Nothing is open, just the take-out cafe." At that moment, a young African man came up the stairs, and recognized Uncle Sam. They chatted for a few minutes, and I asked, "Do you know a sit-down place to eat nearby?"

The young man answered, "Go down these stairs, and there is a restaurant open." I sighed with relief. We walked down several stairs, and saw the restaurant with a large out-door patio. Uncle Sam moved several times, from the inside to outside, looking for the place with the right ambience for talking— something I do all the time. I felt an affinity with him, as if we were friends from a past life.

We finally found a large table overlooking the ocean, and Uncle Sam ordered an omelette with all the sides and I ordered a fruit plate. I opened my notebook.

"Close that book and open your ears and just listen!" he scolded me. "White people don't listen. We have met many writers, and they take all these notes and go away back home. And then the book is nothing like what we hoped or expected. They tell us it was their publishers who made them change the words. We have talked to writers before, and the book then took a radical turn, so we are very cautious.

"You need to treat this subject respectfully. You are writing history from the Royal Hawaiian point of view. You are getting the advice of generational experts like myself. Do not take a critical tone, do not be derogatory about the European visitors."

I thought to myself, how can I not be derogatory, when every history book I had read focused on lines taken out of context from the early journals? Stereotypes about naked natives trading everything away for trinkets, captains and officers who were stiff disciplinarians, military men working for the Crown, empty lands waiting to be colonized. Yet here was a respected indigenous elder, telling me to not be critical of the Europeans. I had to honour his request. There had been so much written about the natives in history textbooks that was inaccurate, biased and coming from a prejudiced point of view. Uncle Sam was right: it was time to take a different approach. Two wrongs don't make a right.

I closed my notebook, desperately hoping I would remember and honour his words from memory.

"We had no concept of original sin, and the word 'own' did not exist in our dictionary. We thought we were giving the land to share. We were sharing the fruits, not giving away the soil and the roots. Our genealogy prior to late 1700s is based on oral history. Oral history is more accurate to us than the written word. Once you release the words, you cannot take it back. It is a contract between you and the Creator."

Uncle Sam told me the missionaries misunderstood the Hawaiian concept of God. "They needed one God. We believe in Io. Io does not have to care. He is plasma, gravity, the high and low tide, the seasons, the moon, the sun. It is the breath in and out. Io is everything.

"The missionaries said that if Io does not care, it cannot be God. We told them, Io does not give advice. He is the ancient murmuring that speaks before the storm will engulf you."

As I listened to him talk, I realized that Sam Kaha'i Kaai was a gifted poet, to rival Shakespeare. Yet, he had not written down his words; he shared that he was dyslexic, had difficulty writing and was not comfortable with people writing while he spoke.

When I returned to my hotel at the end of the day, I went to the Napili Bay beach, to reflect on Uncle Sam's words. I walked into the ocean, which was heaving slowly like a massive whale restlessly deciding to turn this way or that. I decided to float on top of the water and meditate. In and out—breathe in and out. Io was all around me, I was one with the ocean, with the light. It was an incredibly peaceful feeling, yet powerful at the same time. I let my will go, and surrendered to the magical ocean around me. I thought about Uncle Sam's words: "There is close vision, far vision and peripheral vision. Do you have peripheral vision, Mary?"

I recalled Uncle Sam saying that some people may challenge me for publishing previously hidden stories. I thought, we have come too far to stop now. I felt all these officers, royal ladies, kings and chiefs clamouring to be heard. If not us, then who? Wade and I are almost 60. If not now, then when? The box has been shut so tightly for so many years. Misconceptions, prejudices, hidden agendas. Who is the real Captain Vancouver? Was he a visionary ahead of his time? Is it possible he may have been a Master Mason? Captain Cook has been often referred to as a Freemason, although no proof of his membership is available. Is it possible that Captain Vancouver's elegant and respectful descriptions of the women he was meeting fit the Freemasons' view of women at the time. I felt a great kinship with him, a sense of empathy.

Uncle Sam said to me, when I called him to update him on our research in April, 2014, "Oh, you are just awed by that high royal court English style of writing, very respectful and gracious," he said, gently mocking me in his melodious Hawaiian voice. "Only one percent of people at the time knew how to write like that. He would have had private tutors." However, he was very pleased when I shared with him later Captain Vancouver's descriptions of the Hula and the Royal women.

Wade and I visited Uncle Sam at his home in Makawao, Maui, in December, 2014. We sat together and enjoyed a traditional tea and dried banana fruit. He listened as I read the passages to him.

"This is very important information," he said, "that Captain Vancouver recorded accurately the royal demeanour of our women. The true spirit of Aloha. The true meaning of Aloha is the presence of divine breath. I acknowledge the divinity in me, and the divinity in you."

I was amazed at Uncle Sam's knowledge, and how he was the cultural keeper of his people's knowledge, going back hundreds of years. He was like a computer, generations of oral knowledge downloaded into his cells. But he was also wise and understanding. When I told him about our experience with Maureen, at the BC Archives, he said, "Why are you picking on her? She was just doing her job."

I wondered again why he was willing to talk to me. He did not seem the type of person who wasted his time with strangers—he did not suffer fools gladly.

Wade understood. "He talked to you because he knows you will not slant and discard important information. You do not have willful blindness about these matters, and you are willing to hear the hard truths without becoming too emotional and dramatic. He can read people. They were great navigators of the oceans, and they learned to read people as they could read the oceans."

When I told Uncle Sam that we had learned that Captain Vancouver's original journals had disappeared, he said, "They were likely destroyed because the prejudiced English admiralty at the time were horrified by what Captain Vancouver was saying, It would have been blasphemy at the time."

Wade and I were beginning to see the big picture of what

had happened. Lt. Joseph Baker made a note in his Remarks of the Day on July 1, 1795: "The Admiralty order for that purpose being—The Maps and Journals of the officers and the ships company, are demanded by Captain Vancouver for the inspection of their Lordships." Throughout his logbooks, Lt. Baker, with very few exceptions, showed no emotion. Was this because he anticipated that what he wrote would be sent to the Lords of the Admiralty, and he was protecting himself?

This was interesting because they are still at sea at that time and not due to return to England until the early fall. Wade believed that the Admiralty sent out a schooner to pick up the journals from the *Discovery* at sea, before the ship landed in England, to ensure they could confiscate them, or edit them before the Captain and crew returned.

We had read how open, detailed and respectful Captain Vancouver was in his journals. His forward-thinking views would have been out-of-step with the class-consciousness and political agendas in England at the time. As we researched further, we learned about the attempts to discredit Captain Vancouver. There were the Royal Navy "experts" and the Lords of the Admiralty, and no one ever questioned them.

CHAPTER 18

The Line in the Sand, Vancouver, 1792

*Two of the friendly people expressed a desire to pass
the line of separation drawn between us, and were
permitted to do so.*

CAPTAIN GEORGE VANCOUVER

I n contrast to his encounters with the indigenous people
of the Sandwich Islands, Captain Vancouver writes
in far less detail of his time on the Pacific Northwest
Coast. However, he does write in some detail about the
social and trading protocols of their relationship with the
First Nations people they encountered. And it was this
social interaction that led to the marriage of Lt. Baker and
Princess Capilano.

May, 1792 In the course of the forenoon on Friday,
25th May some of our Indian friends brought us a
whole deer, which was the first entire animal that had

been offered to us. This they had killed on the island, and from the number of persons that that came from thence, the major part of the remaining inhabitants of the village, with a great number of their dogs, seemed to have even engaged in chase. This and another deer, parts of which remained in one of their canoes, had cost all these good people nearly a days labour, as they went over to the island for this purpose the preceding evening; yet they were amply rewarded for their exertions by by a small piece of copper not a foot square. This they gladly accepted as full compensation for their venison, on which the whole party could have made two or three meals: such is the esteem and value with which this metal is regarded.

Captain Vancouver goes on to describe their character as marked by "their readiness to assert what they think is most agreeable in the moment."

Wade agreed that many people misinterpret this Coast Salish trait of appearing agreeable and pleasant at first. "They need thinking time to deliberate the true value of the situation. They are agreeing to look at the situation. There are several steps before concluding."

May, 1792 About a dozen of these friendly people… attended at our dinner, one part of which was a venison pasty. Two of them, expressing a desire to pass the line of separation drawn between us, were permitted to do so. They sat down by us, and ate of the bread and fish that we gave them without the least hesitation; but on being offered some of the venison, though they saw us eat it with great relish, they could not be induced to taste it. They received it from us with great disgust, and presented it round to the rest of the party, by whom it underwent a very strict examination. Their conduct on this occasion left no doubt in our minds that they believed it to be human flesh, and refused to eat it. This led us to conclude that the character given of the natives of Northwest America does not attach to every tribe.

To satisfy them that it was the flesh of the deer, we pointed to the skins of the animals they had about them. In reply to this, they pointed to each other, and made signs that could not be misunderstood, that it was the flesh of human beings, and threw it down into the dirt, with gestures of great aversion and displeasure. At length, we happily convinced them of their mistake by showing them a haunch we had in the boat, by which means they were undeceived, and some of them ate of the remainder of the pye with a good appetite.

It appears that the saying "draw a line in the sand" may come from this practice of drawing a line in the sand, with the captain and officers sitting on one side and the chiefs and their entourage on the other side. They would sit and discuss the protocol of the visit, and how things should unfold over the next few days or weeks.

May, 1792 Having landed about 9 o clock to break-fast, and to take advantage of the sun and wind to dry some of our clothes, our friends, the Indians, seventeen in numbers, landed also from six canoes about half a mile ahead of us, and then walked towards our party, attended by a single canoe along the shore; having hauled up all the others. They now approached us with the utmost confidence, without being armed, and behaved in the most respectful, orderly manner. On a line being drawn with a stick on the sand between the two parties, they immediately sat down, and no one attempted to pass it, without previously making signs requesting permission for so doing.

We then paddled towards their village which was situated in a very pleasant cove , a little to the SW, and built with wood... the Indians who visited with us this morning, bringing with them small square boxes filled with fresh water, which we could not tempt them to dispose of.

These good people conducted themselves in the most friendly manner. They had little to dispose of, yet they bartered away their bows and arrows without the least hesitation, together with some small fish, cockles and clams; of the latter we purchased a large quantity... We then proceeded to a large point of land that forms the north entrance into the cove. There we beheld a large number of the natives, the whole assembly seated quietly on the grass, excepting two or three whose particular office seemed to be to welcome us to their country.

They presented us with some fish, and received in return some trinkets of various kinds... we were received by them with equal cordiality and treated with marks of great friendship and hospitality.

This country is capable of great potential for agriculture, and productions grow in equal luxuriance with those under similar parallels in Europe.

The following year, when Captain Vancouver and his crew return to the northwest coast of America, the protocols of trading are in place and understood.

September, 1793 Early the next morning, Ononnistay, attended by all the other chiefs, came off in his large canoe, and according to their custom, sang while they paddled around the vessels.

This ceremony being ended, they came alongside the *Discovery*, and exhibited a kind of entertainment, humorous and exaggerated.

I had not before witnessed this type of ceremony. It consisted of singing and a display of extravagant gestures. The principal parts were performed by the Chiefs, each in succession becoming the leader or hero of the song. At each of the pauses. I was presented with a sea otter skin. After the parts were played, they desired to be admitted on board. Ononnistay gave us to understand, that, as peace and goodwill were now established, he wished that trading might be allowed. This taking place accordingly, several sea otter skins, a great number of salmon, and various trivial articles were purchased. Fire arms and ammunition were first demanded, on reconciling our refusal they entered into a brisk traffic for blue cloth, files and tin kettles which they preferred next to firearms, in exchange for their sea otter skins. Their fish and less valuable articles were readily parted with for pewter spoons, looking glasses, beads and other trinkets. The party of Indians thus assembled amounted to about 50 persons, who conducted themselves with strict honesty and much propriety.

The Indians inquired if it was our intention to visit their abode, and I replied in the affirmative. This appeared to give them much pleasure.

Wade told me that it is very common in longhouse ceremonies to have an element of humour, and that it is also used in formal welcoming ceremonies to this day. It is apparent that there was very strict protocol in a welcoming ceremony and humorous interaction before any trading commenced to set a tone of goodwill.

June, 1792 The Chief, a middle-aged man, was foremost in showing us marks of the greatest hospitality; and perceiving our party was at breakfast, presented them with water, roasted roots, dried fish, and other articles of food. This person, in return, received some presents. And others were distributed amongst the ladies and some of the party... They appeared to have not before seen Europeans... Most of the good people took their leave, and seemed to part with their newly acquired friends with great reluctance.

This last comment made me wonder if this passage had been edited, as Captain Vancouver always named the chiefs with detailed descriptions in his other writings. We assume this may have been either Chief Capilano or Chief Paytsmuck.

June, 1792 Some of the natives we met with, who differed not, in any material particular, as to their persons nor in their civil and hospitable deportment, from those we had been so happy, on former occasions to call our friends…

I had absented myself from the present surveying excursions in order to procure some observations… These, when so methodized, my third lieutenant Mr. Baker had undertaken to copy and embellish, and who, in point of accuracy, neatness, and such dispatch as circumstances admitted, certainly excelled in a very high degree.

ON MAY 27, 2014, I returned to the Vancouver Maritime Museum to recheck some dates in the journals. Lindsay at the front desk turned to Allan, and said, "Mary is going to be working here soon, she is here so much."

I smiled and said, "Yes I am cross checking some dates to be sure it is accurate what I am writing down."

"That is good," Lindsay replied.

Lea was waiting for me when I came back from putting the parking notice on my car. As we walked downstairs, I asked her, "Is there any way to find out what the real Captain Vancouver looked like?"

"Let me think about it," she said, and laid the first journal out for me. I was surrounded by nude mannequins, which Lea explained were for an upcoming swimsuit exhibit. Lea returned to her office, and I sat down and started chatting with Sarah, my PhD researcher friend, who was also at the museum.

"I am just cross-checking some dates, as I don't think anyone has actually read through these journals in entirety."

"Yes, I think they took a very narrow focus," Sarah said. "One book I read said they had limited social interaction for a year prior to landing on June 12 or 13, 1792. Yet, in March they were socializing regularly in Hawaii with various royal and other personages."

Another history book from June 1954, describes the events in June as follows.

On June 13th, 1792, at 4:00 am they sailed again. They saw but did not explore the entrance to Indian Arm, and passed through Second Narrows, the main Harbour and First Narrows… Few of the Indians were up; two canoes put out from the beach at First Narrows, but could not catch Vancouver's boats which had a fresh favourable breeze.[9]

Here is how Captain Vancouver writes about this same event in his journal.

June, 1792 Thursday, June 14th, 1792. Perfectly satisfied with our researches in this branch of the sound, at four the next morning, we retraced our passage in; leaving on the northern shore, a small opening extending to the northward with two little islets before it of little importance, whilst we had a grander object in contemplation; and more particularly so, as this arm or canal could not be deemed navigable for shipping. The tide caused no stream; the Colour of its water after we had passed the island the day before, was perfectly clear, whereas that in the main branch of the sound, extending nearly half over the gulf, and accompanied by a rapid tide, was nearly colourless, which gave us some reason to suppose that the northern branch of the sound might possibly be discovered to terminate in a river of considerable extent.

As we passed the situation whence the Indians had first visited us the preceding day, which is a small border of marshy land on the northern shore, intersected by several creeks of fresh water, we were in expectation of their company, but were disappointed, owing to our travelling so soon in the morning. Most of their canoes were hauled up into the creeks, and two or three only of the natives were seen straggling about on the beach. None of their habitations could be discovered, whence we concluded that their village was within the forest. Two canoes came off as we passed the Island, but our boats being under sail, with a fresh favourable breeze, I was not inclined to halt, and they almost immediately returned.

Captain Vancouver then continues his description of sailing through Howe Sound and trading with the indigenous people they met.

June, 1792 The gap we had entered in the snowy barrier seemed of little importance, as through the valleys caused by the irregularity of the mountain's tops; other mountains were distant, and apparently more elevated, were seen rearing their lofty heads in various directions. In this dreary and comfortless region, it was so inconsiderable a piece of good fortune to find a little cove in which we could take shelter, and a small spot of level land on which we could erect our tent; as we had scarcely finished our examination, when the wind became excessively boisterous from the southward, attended with heavy squalls and torrents of rain which continuing until noon the following day, occasioned a very unpleasant detention. But for this circumstance, we might too hastily have concluded, that this part of the gulf was uninhabited. In the morning, we were visited by near forty of the natives, on whose approach, from the very material alteration that had now taken place in the face of the country, we expected to find some difference in their general character. This conjecture was however, premature, as they varied in no respect whatever, but in possessing a more ardent desire for commercial transactions; into the spirit of which they entered with infinitely more avidity than any of our former, not only in bartering amongst themselves the different valuables they had obtained from us, but when that trade became slack, in exchanging those articles again with our people; in which traffic they always took care to gain some advantage, and would frequently exult on the occasion. Some fish, their garments, spears, bows and arrows, to which these people wisely added to their copper ornaments, comprised their general stock in trade. iron, in all its forms, they judiciously preferred to any other article we had to offer…

June 18th Under the circumstances, our reduced stock of provisions was a matter of serious concern…

The *Discovery* then encounters Spanish ships.

June 22nd, Friday From these new and unexpected friends (Spanish) we directed our course along the shoal already noticed, which I now called Sturgeon Bank, in consequence of our having purchased from the natives some excellent fish of that kind, weighing from fourteen to 200 pounds each.

CHAPTER 19

Stanley Park Longhouse, 1792

I was invited into an Indian Village…

LT. JOSEPH BAKER

On my return to Vancouver from Maui, I had been elated to find out that the First Peoples' Cultural Council had given Wade a grant to research his ancestor, Lt. Joseph Baker. For several years, Wade had managed to keep his illiteracy from me. It was a courageous step to return to high school at the age of 56. Receiving the grant, following on from his amazing presentation for the Arrow-Might learning program, was a validation of his achievement.

Wade had called his project "Alliance Marriages." His oral knowledge was that some of these captains and lieutenants did marry chiefs' daughters in order to ensure that provisions, supplies and friendly trade and social relationships were maintained. The "marriages" may have been a celebration at a feast in the village. Any children from the alliance were looked after by the mother and her family. Oral knowledge is that the fathers often did visit the children when they returned on trade missions and expeditions.

We had to find proof that Lt. Joseph Baker was in a village near Stanley Park at the time that oral history placed him there, and that while he was on land he socialized with the First Nations people .

His logbook does say he was invited into an Indian village in July 1792. However, he mentions very few other details.

July 14th, 1792 Invited into an Indian Village… brought trifling presents.

FOR WADE, THE story of his ancestors' meeting and love match is like a memory:

I noticed a striking-looking young lady standing next to the two chiefs who had earlier greeted them by circling around the ships in their canoes, singing the welcoming song ceremony.

She was wearing a beautiful, woollen white dress. Her bearing reminded me of the noble ladies at the British Court. She had an entourage of waiting ladies around her, who noticed that we were gazing at each other, and eyed me suspiciously.

Later in the evening, the captain turned to me and said:

"Joseph, we have been at sea for many months. I can see you are very restless, and that you feel attracted to the young lady of consequence whom we met earlier with her father, the chief."

I replied, "Yes. When I was out surveying, she was also abroad, with several chaperones. I am emotionally attracted to her and she to me, I am sure. I found out from the interpreter that her name is Kwasan, but as the daughter of the chief, her position must be respected. I cannot be with her as I wish because of the taboo protocols."

The captain looked at me, and thought deeply for a few minutes.

"For practical reasons, I understand. You are unmarried, have highborn features and bearing, and we have been at sea for months. In the eyes of English law, it would not be a legally sanctioned marriage. Yes, we do have unwritten policies about intermarrying. Since the unfortunate circumstances of the *Bounty*, we are more lenient about these matters. For the betterment of the Dominion of England, this alliance would keep peace amongst us. I still remember the chaos of Captain Cook's untimely death. Once you become family, it will create an amiable disposition towards us for future surveying and trading.

"I will speak to the chief tomorrow morning on board ship with our interpreter, and we will proceed. You may stay here for awhile, and continue with the surveying. I will tell the officers you need to continue your work, and that we are leaving you here as we have other tasks to attend to. You can meet up with us in Nootka before we proceed back to Owaghee. You must know that on our return to England, at the end of the voyage, you will have to marry and settle down."

I thanked the captain for his plan, and responded with respect. "But I wish to see Kwasan each time we return here for the summer months. I know her person, and she is a companion to my soul. I feel at peace when I am with her. She is so different from the restricted and closed women I know in England, only concerned with social status and the opinions of their class."

The chief arranged our marriage at the longhouse, and the blanket of security was placed around myself and Kwasan. It was a private ceremony witnessed by only my captain, the chiefs and their royal entourage.

WADE BELIEVES THAT he may have inherited many traits passed down to him from his British ancestor.

"I am not affected by the weather. We were very clean, having spiritual baths every day in the cold water. So the rest of the day felt warm. This would have been very appealing to the British, who came from an environment where many did not bathe for weeks.

"I have a perfectionism about details, spending hours on my drawings: everything has to be orderly. Lt. Baker was an artist, but he was also in charge of keeping the decks cleaned and was used to telling people what to do and having his orders followed. I used to bark out orders, and expect people to jump, but I have mellowed around that. My mind has a very organized format; when I am doing a project, I am also organizing.

"I also like to collect antique crystal gentlemen's toiletry items for a gentleman's personal use. I also can be very stubborn and single-minded when I want something, and am also very loyal. My writing is very tight and uniform. It all merges together, very similar to his writing style.

"I can also be lethargic at times, then suddenly have this great urge for action, and I am very good at setting up camp wherever I go."

SINCE WADE WAS in full-time attendance at school, studying for his high school diploma, I continued the research on his behalf going through Captain Vancouver's three journals.

We knew that the original of Captain Vancouver's journal had disappeared, but other references referred to the surviving letters of Archibald Menzies, a naturalist on board the *Discovery* during the 1791–1795 expeditions, which hinted at attempts to discredit Vancouver on his return to England. He appears to have been shunned by the Admiralty in England, and was never again given a ship to command. Captain Vancouver died less than three years later, having arrived back to London in perfect health.

Wade's journey to discover the story of his ancestor Lt. Joseph Baker, kept leading us back to the story of Captain Vancouver, the mystery of his vanished journals and his untimely death.

Captain Vancouver has detailed descriptions of the dress, personalities and events in Hawaii, Monterrey and San Francisco, yet his journal entries for the Pacific Northwest Coast appear curt with very little detail or names of the native peoples, other than their expertise at trading. It is very mysterious and vague, and very likely edited, as it is markedly different from the writing style for entries about the other areas he visited.

CHAPTER 20

Oral History and Language

Oral tradition is not about words, but formulating
thought and discarding what is not important.

KAHU DAVID KAPAKU

Wade was learning about his Squamish oral language at the Eslahan Learning Centre, and was told that if even one word was remembered wrong, you would be called a liar.

According to Wade, First Nations' oral language was so precise that the story was never altered or changed in any way. The Europeans, with their perspective, could not understand this. In their view, stories would change as different persons told it, resulting in a complete misunderstanding between the two cultures.

"Do you remember when you would read bedtime stories to Sierra when she was four or five, and she would get very upset if you changed or skipped parts of the story in any way because of tiredness," Wade asked me. "Even at that young age, she knew the story must not be changed. She would look at you with that very serious expression and say, 'Mum, don't change the story.'"

While I had been in Maui, I went to a cultural talk given by oral history expert Kahu David Kapaku at The Ritz-Carlton, Kapalua hotel. He agreed to speak with me privately.

Minister David explained that oral tradition cannot be argued, because everyone sees the same thing. The words describe visual pictures. Oral tradition is not about words, but formulating thoughts and about discarding what is not important. The heart of oral tradition is, what is important? For example, if one says "Good morning" in English, people see a hundred different images in their mind, from sitting with coffee on the verandah, to rising from bed, to going for that first walk, to going to a café to buy a coffee and pastry, etc.

"*Ka Kahi aka* in Hawaiian means 'The First Shadow.' Then, everyone sees the same picture in their mind. They don't have to imagine it.

"Take the word 'sustainability.' The word *aina* means land in Hawaiian, and to feed many. If you think in Hawaiian, the land is the chief, and we are the servants. Hawaii is not power-based, but land-based.

UNCLE SAM HAD suggested I speak also with Clifford Naeole, who is the cultural advisor at The Ritz-Carlton hotel.

"This is the time of passing on the knowledge," Uncle Sam said to me when I asked why the elders were willing to speak to me.

As soon as I returned to my unit, I phoned the hotel and

spoke to Clifford, who immediately understood the research we were doing. "Oh, you are writing about the time of the to and fro," he said, "when the waves were just meeting the shore, the transition period?"

I told him I had just met with Sam Kahaʻi Kaai. "Oh, you went to the Source? Sam K is a Hawaiian cultural practitioner, a Kupuna. He is a keeper of the knowledge."

"Yes," I said, "and I was scolded. I have also been scolded for 20 years by my husband's First Nations' community, and scolded by my own family as well."

I have come to realize that all this scolding has helped me as a writer, as I can allow people to state their opinions without becoming defensive or leading the conversation.

Clifford said to me, "You can wear those bruises as badges of honour. The white people have a lot to learn, they do not listen."

"Sam told me to close my notebook. Not to write, just listen," I said.

"Yes, close the book, open your ears, and you will hear," Clifford agreed. He then offered to buy me breakfast the next morning, and take me on a tour of the Wahi Pana (sacred site) behind the hotel.

The next day, I went to meet Clifford as arranged. I walked past dozens of palm trees and saw beautiful plumeria flowers cascading down terraces and arbours after I had parked the rental car. It was difficult to find the lobby, because The Ritz-Carlton is a low-rise hotel designed to fit into the undulating landscape. The lobby, when I eventually found it, overlooked the ocean, with many different seating areas and low tables for reading and refreshments. Long sheer white curtains moved softly with the constant warm tropical breezes from the open doorways. Pineapples and ancient Hawaiian motifs were engraved and carved into the furniture and chandeliers. Fans slowly moved overhead. A waiter came over and asked if I would like some tea while I waited.

Clifford then walked over to me and ushered me into the restaurant which was still busy with guests finishing up at the breakfast buffet. He had a noble and highborn demeanour. He seemed confident in his chosen profession, knowing he had made a difference to his people. We settled into a quiet corner. I could see that Clifford was very well respected as several waiters came over to ensure he was comfortable.

Clifford started speaking, and I was honoured that he felt at ease with me.

"When did the Hawaiian sense of Aloha, acceptance and welcome become a sign of weakness to the other side?" he asked me. "Our traditions of hospitality, acceptance and welcome made Hawaii too easy to sell."

Clifford spoke of Kuleana, responsibility. "Something to lead, something to write, it is in the blood," he said. "My ancestors were also Ali'i, royalty. Prior to the birth of King Kamehameha I, the Kahuna foretold that a child will be born who will be above all. When Kamehameha was born, there was the sign of the white comet. This signified someone who would be of high importance. The high priests and chiefs, through their fear of a future power struggle, created a plot to kill the baby. To protect the child, he was given to a different father to raise. He was given to my ancestor, Chief Naeole, who hid him in the hills for ten years. At 15 years old, Kamehameha was already very tall and strong, and could lift the Naha stone. Everyone fought for the ear of the 'Lonely One.'"

Uncle Sam had also called King Kamehameha the "Lonely One."

"He is called that because a true leader or chief listens to all the people, then makes the decision on his own. The king leads for the idea. He is the one who does not give advice, he receives it. He decides on the life and death of people. That is what makes him the 'Lonely One,'" Uncle Sam had explained to me.

Clifford also knew about the strong friendship between Captain Vancouver and the local Hawaiians. I asked about what would have happened to any children who may have been produced from relationships with the ships' officers. He said that the babies would have belonged to the mothers, and that in tribal customs, it would not be unusual to have several mothers or fathers.

"What was important was, are you authentic, are you a good citizen? The missionaries said that any marriages not blessed by the church meant you were living in sin. Only the first wife of King Kamehameha I was registered, Queen Ka'ahumanu, even though Kamehameha II had 30 wives, for example. He died in 1890. The missionaries would not have recorded any marriages between officers and royal daughters. This oral knowledge has all been ignored by official state history. By 1840 to 1850, there were 500 whaling ships off the coast of Lahaina. There was piracy by paper and force of arms," Clifford related.

Hawaiian language expert Kahu David Kapaku had told us that 200 years prior to Captain Cook, the Hawaiians knew about the Europeans as they travelled back and forth to Polynesia, and had met the early Spanish explorers. Queen Kaʻahumanu, King Kamehameha's favourite wife, knew about the missionary movement in Tahiti, because the master navigators brought back all the up-to-date information. "There were 1300 to 1500 temples on Maui prior to western contact," David had explained.

"Things set in motion by law produces bitter fruit," Clifford continued. "We realized that the god of these people does not favour us, and the European concept of anti-dark came to our islands. 1850 to 1950: was that period of 'worldwide culture' that marginalized us."

CHAPTER 21

Hale Pa'i Museum, Maui

I was incredibly excited. Wade and I had suspected that there were strong relationships between Captain Vancouver and the officers and the Hawaiians, and now we had proof from two highly respected cultural elders who had agreed to speak with me, passing on their very detailed oral knowledge of the times.

So, why was very little of this written in the history books of the past century?

I asked Uncle Sam. He said Captain Vancouver did write this down, however his family was horrified, and his words were ignored by official British history and the Admiralty. Captain Vancouver's writings were contrary to the popular thought of what a "savage" was.

"That is why the original journals were destroyed or missing," Uncle Sam said. "He would have been declared persona non grata if he did not go along with the official position. He died of remorse and being excluded. A peer of the realm owns the realm. Nobility was not supposed to work in the official sense. The lands (colonial territories) claimed by the British king would have been dispersed to the realm, given to the nobility. Possibly the French museums may have unedited copies.

"The first generation of missionaries was kind, but the second generation, their sons, took the land. These sons returned from their American universities with ideas that exploited the Hawaiians."

After meeting with Uncle Sam and Clifford Naeole, I finally went to the Hale Pa'i print museum at the Lahainaluna High School, driving up a long dusty road, passing a Hawaiian war canoe on the way, which was perched on the left side of the road. I parked in the high school parking lot, and wandered around until I found the small museum hidden behind some trees.

It was deserted, except for the docent, Chi Pilialoha, who was on duty that day. I could immediately see that the preservation of Hawaiian oral history and culture was very important to her. She had a kind and caring manner that put me immediately at ease. I introduced myself to her, and she gave me a pair of soft cotton gloves. Then she kindly allowed me to rummage through the dusty shelves and their untidy piles of books. I settled in for a long, hot day of research, the fans slowly turning above me.

I asked Chi, "What do you think they were doing when they were not on the ships?" She answered, "They were drinking," and I realized she was talking about the whaling ships, not the *Discovery*.

Trusting my finely tuned sense of intuition, I chose the shelves closest to her desk. That's where the most interesting papers would be found, I thought. Otherwise, I knew I would be there for days, with little hope of finding anything other than old choir books and yearbooks. I did find an interesting pamphlet from June, 1831, titled "The Assembly of the General Meeting of Hawaiian Missionaries, Honolulu."

Resolved that we consider the education of these islands generally and the preparation of some of them in particular for becoming the teachers of religion, as holding a great importance in our missionary work.

A score of AYES resounded through the narrow confines of the meeting house.

The AYES have it, responded the Chairman. With the adoption of that resolution, higher education was born in Hawaii.

Later in the pamphlet, there was this passage:

And in connection with the foregoing, it is also the design of this institution to disseminate sound knowledge throughout these islands, embracing literature and the sciences, and whatever may tend eventually to elevate the whole mass of the people from their present ignorance, that they may become a thinking, enlightened and virtuous people. And also to train native school teachers for their respective duties, to teach them theoretically and practically the best methods of communicating instruction to others. From these horrible beginnings, Hawaii's system of higher education was born.

I then learned about the Doctrine of Discovery, which was expounded in the United States Supreme Court in 1823. With its roots in 15th-century Papal bulls regarding Portuguese and Spanish colonization of new lands, the Discovery Doctrine stated that the title to any land occupied by non-European, non-Christians could be claimed by the government whose subjects had visited and occupied those lands. The indigenous people who lived there, under the Discovery Doctrine, had no sovereignty or property rights; the "discovering nation" could claim the land from the natives through conquest or "purchase."

These laws were embedded in the consciousness of colonial nations for centuries, and were used to justify heinous acts of conquest.

Learning this, I realized that anything published after 1830 would likely have this superior attitude: boring and repetitive in its smugness at the best, soul-destroying at the worst.

I needed to focus my search on that far more interesting and complex time period between 1790 and 1820.

I willed any documents from that time period to jump off the shelves. Chi had no inventory system, explaining that the computers were down and the new system had lost all the old archival information.

I did find an interesting version of the Young and Davis story, which Uncle Sam had told me about, in an 1898 journal.

At the time of the late 1700s, the American trading vessels were getting away with trading one nail for one pig from the Hawaiians. King Kamehameha realized that he needed help to negotiate with the Americans. Captain Metcalf of the Eleanor had killed one hundred natives in retaliation for a native stealing a small boat. In revenge, a Kona Chief, Kameeiamoku captured the Eleanor's sister ship, the Fair American, which was under the command of Captain Metcalf's son. Kameeiamoku killed all the crew on board except the mate, Isaac Davis, whose life he spared. The vessel was hauled ashore and all the guns and powder taken to Kamehameha. That same day, John Young, boatswain, of the Eleanor, had been wandering around on shore, and was taken prisoner. One story is that Young and Davis were treated very kindly. Kamehameha gave them rich lands, and made them both chiefs. They, in return, served him faithfully in war and peace. Both know how to use firearms and cannons, and they trained Kamehameha's army in the use of muskets. Now, with the guns ... captured from the Fair American, together with the two white men, Young and Davis as leaders, Kamehameha was ready to begin the war to unite the islands. He planned first to take Maui.[10]

This same article went on to explain what was considered to be behaviour worthy of a chief.

The Chief was to have complete knowledge of war, government, the laws of the kingdom, and the rules of tabu.

Matched with other Chiefs for ten days in trials of strength and skill before thousands of people. He outran the fastest both on the plain, and in bringing a snowball from the top of Mauna Koa. On a level plain, he leaped the length of two long war spears. In a canoe race he outdistanced all the others, then plunged into the sea with a pahoa in his hand, and slew and brought to the surface, the body of a large shark. He caught in his hands 20 spears thrown at him, one after another, by 20 strong arms, and cast to the ground all the chiefs he had wrestled.[11]

CHAPTER 22

Madame Rose, France, 1817

I do not regret hiding myself on my husband's
ship… it was the best time of my life.

MADAME ROSE DE SAULCES DE FREYCINET

I sat in the Lahainaluna Print Museum, hot and frustrated, and decided to go outside for some fresh air and to think. I remembered Uncle Sam saying that the French might have had a different attitude towards the islanders. I went back to the shelves behind Chi again, and started carefully looking at the books on the third shelf down. Something made me pick up a book with its cover torn off. The inside page read, in French:

Journal de Madame Rose de Saulces de Freycinet
Gibraltar, Teneriffe, les Canarries
Campagne de l'Uranie
1817–1820

Here at least was the time period I was interested in. In a desultory manner, I flipped through the pages and, suddenly, came across an astonishing sketch. I looked closer, and realized the sketch showed young native men, wearing officers' jackets. I quickly did the math in my mind, and tried to contain my excitement. These would be the children of the 1790s officers. They must have left their jackets for the women to give to their sons when they were older.

I quickly took as many photos as I could of the pages. There was no explanation of the sketches. Many were of obviously mixed-race young ladies and men of high status. Others were of European officers comfortably at home with the natives. Chi looked over, worried, and reminded me not to use a flash. Something told me to be cautious about what I had found. This was a journal of amazing importance, discarded on a dusty shelf. These were detailed observations from a women's point of view, of all the many local persons she met with her husband on the various islands.

Madame Rose was born Rose Marie Pinon on September 29, 1794, in St. Julien de Sault in France. She was married at the age of 20, on June 6, 1814, in Paris to Louis Claude de Saulces de Freycinet, a ship's captain. In 1817, he was given the command of the *Uranie*, for a three-year world scientific exploration.

Several days after the *Uranie* departed Toulon, the Minister realized that Madame Rose was missing, and had likely been hidden aboard her husband's ship. She had been observed accompanying her husband to the departure, and then disappeared soon after. Women were not allowed at the time to accompany their husbands. The Minister wrote to the Maritime Prefect at Toulon and the Gibraltar Consul to demand an explanation, however the *Uranie* had already been long gone, and the telegraph had yet to arrive!

I realized I had to read the text to see if I could find any references to Captain Vancouver's visits to the islands, and started to laboriously translate the old French language. I was pleased that my years of training in French at university, and that summer in Switzerland, were finally paying off. After a few pages, it became easier to read.

On, August 8, 1819, Madame Rose met John Adams in the Sandwich Islands. Uncle Sam had given me detailed information about John Adams, who was one of King Kamehameha I's advisors.

Madame Rose had written:

His name was Kaiouva, but he had taken the English name of John Adams. He was about 30 years old... about six feet, three inches in height, a true colossus. I had never seen a man so tall and big. He spoke very good English, and he instructed Louis extensively in Geography. I never expected this from a savage, even from a prince, and we had many useful, informative conversations.

Her entry, two days later:

Today, we invited John Adams for dinner, also intending to give him some presents. To our grand surprise, he brought his wife Keohoua, and one of her friends. I will describe her. She was about 30 years old, five feet ten inches in height... Both wore beautiful earrings and necklaces.

On August 12, 1819, she writes of the ship's visit to "Koaihai Bay, Island of Owighee."

Louis received a deputation in the morning on behalf of the Sandwich Island Majesty who waited for us on land impatiently... Louis went onto the land with the brother of John Adams, and another young Frenchman. If I can, I will give a history of the reception. We had read Captain Vancouver's journals about his relationship with the old King Tamaahmah [Kamehameha] and it is unfortunate he has passed away. Louis was hoping that this circumstance would not make our approaches too difficult.

August 13, 1819

The King, wearing a grand costume of an English Captain, waited for Louis on the beach, in front of his house. His wives were not far away, under a light canopy for shade. The King ordered his cannons to be shot to welcome and honour our visit. After that, with a small movement of his head, he nodded to Louis to invite him into his house.

Eight years after her return, she wrote that she did not regret what she did, as life is so short. She passed away at 38 years old.

Madame Rose's journals offered very different information from traditional historical records written by the majority of men: longitude and latitude readings, and numbers of cannons, reports of wars, etc. These men completely ignored the social interactions, except for a sentence or two, but here was detailed, daily information about friendships and contacts. Madame Rose wanted me to share her story—I saw her sitting a few feet away from me in the museum, full floor-length skirts arranged around her, mischievously smiling at me, her petite ankles crossed. I promised her I would write her story, as soon as Wade and I had finished *The Hidden Journals.*

I was amazed that it was common knowledge then in Europe at the time about Captain Vancouver's strong relationships with the locals. Yet, the official 21st-century Hawaiian take on the islands' history seemed to generally stop with Captain Cook. Why had Captain Vancouver been airbrushed out of current interpretation of that time period of history?

This seemed very odd to me. I thought to myself: Mary, you are not seeing something. Why has Captain Cook been extensively written about and recorded when he was in Hawaii for only three months, and died there? Captain Vancouver had been there for three years, on and off, but there was only very brief mention of him in colonial written history—at least in the Maui museums.

CHAPTER 23

Old Lahaina Court and Custom House

History is a novel, a fairy tale, a contrivance of the mind. What I do has a rhythm 1500 years long.

SAM KAHAʻI KAAI

The historical panels at the Old Lahaina Court and Custom House museum, built in 1859 during the reign of Kamehameha IV, show a historical timeline of the islands, starting with the ancient myths. I spent an entire day in the museum trying to find even a nugget of information about Captain Vancouver. Under a stern portrait of Captain Cook in 1778, is the description: "British Captain James Cook. This is the islands' first contact with the western world."

The next panel to the right shows an elderly King Kamehameha I. Next to his portrait on the timeline: "1802 to 1803, King Kamehameha I builds war canoe fleet in Lahaina. 1810, King Kamehameha I rules the islands. 1819. King

A PERSONAL JOURNEY OF DISCOVERY

Kamehameha I dies, and the kapu system is discarded by King Kamehameha II. [This is the king whom Madame Rose met in 1819.] 1820. Whaling ships begin visiting Lahaina, bringing commerce and sometimes chaos."

Why was the entire period from 1779 to 1800 ignored? Lt. Joseph Baker's mapping of the Sandwich Islands was used for the next 100 years, a significant accomplishment. This made no sense to me. I returned to the Court and Custom House museum in Lahaina the next day, and spent several hours again going through the rooms to see if I had missed anything. I stopped at every single painting, artifact and written commentary about the historical timeline, and took photos as well to ensure I was not inadvertently missing something. I went over all the timeline panels a second and third time, starting with the ancient Hawaiian creation myth.

It was very quiet in the museum; all the tourists were outside under the banyan tree, shopping for souvenirs, eating lunch at the Colonial Inn, or watching the parrots and vendors on the street. I was relieved, as I am sure my behaviour would have looked strange to a casual observer. One man came back into the room and saw me looking at the original Hawaiian flag hanging on the wall. I recalled Uncle Sam telling me that the flag was a hybrid of the British flag and the American: eight stripes representing the eight islands. The British flag was special to the Hawaiians, as it was Captain Vancouver who worked with the British government to create a treaty to protect the Big Island from the Americans and other interests. The treaty was never ratified, but King Kamehameha I was allowed to fly the British Red Ensign, up until the war of 1812.

The man looked suspiciously at me again, perhaps thinking I was a little too intent on the flag and exhibits. I was wondering if he was a security guard, and tried to act a little more casual, just a cultural tourist interested in the old royalty. He finally left to go downstairs.

I returned to the Hale Pa'i Print Museum the next afternoon to see if I could find any more information. However, the museum was closed.

ON DECEMBER 16, 2013, my daughter and I were invited to The Ritz-Carlton to watch a documentary about Hawaiian history in the hotel theatre called *Then There Were None*, by Dr. Elizabeth Kapu'uwailani Lindsey.

In 1893, the Hawaiian kingdom was overthrown by the descendants of the missionaries and a group of businessmen. There was an unsuccessful counter-revolution, and Queen Lili'uokalani was arrested. President Cleveland directed Congress to restore the Queen to her throne. However, five years later, Hawaii was annexed to the US, and the Queen was forced to sign an abdication. She was dispossessed of her power, rule and lands. Hawaii wept when our flag was lowered.

Clifford elaborated on the documentary. "We became excluded and strangers in our own land. My grandfather was beaten for speaking Hawaiian in school. The missionary children were channelled into arts, letters and the sciences, and groomed for leadership. The Hawaiians were taught farming and home economics. Hollywood built a fantasy of carefree natives around us. The hula was a sacred and spiritual dance.

We had to have a licence that it was only for entertainment purposes, and not a religious practice. Our sacred island of Kahʻolawe was used for target practice by the military.

"The taro patches gave way to hotels and resorts. As the hotels went up, they cordoned off the beaches, so we could not go there any more. The missionaries' children inherited vast tracts of land. The only Hawaiian faces were the royal family, the entertainers and the hotel help. Sugar cane workers were imported from the Philippines, China and Portugal."

When I discussed this with Wade, he said, "The New World order wanted to assimilate or exclude the natives. It was all about taking the world and the land over. The same act was placed onto the natives in the Pacific West Coast. The Indian Act of 1876. The same divide-and-conquer was forced on us here in British Columbia, where we were so busy worrying about who is and is not allowed to be a band member that we did not focus on more important things like education."

Then I thought about what Clifford had told me about the unfair blood quantum law passed 75 years ago. "I was born in 1952 from Hawaiian, Chinese and Caucasian ancestry. There is 80,000 acres of land in Hawaii owned by the state. If you can prove you have over 50 percent pure Hawaiian blood, you can lease the land for 99 years. This has created the 'haves' who are heir to the land, and the 'have nots' who are not heir to the land."

"Are there no lawyers who can take on this outdated law?" I asked Clifford.

"We need to graduate more lawyers," he replied, then abruptly stopped talking.

After a pause, Clifford said, "Let me take you outside to the hotel grounds, and show you our sacred lands." I waited at the front lobby until he finally pulled up in a golf cart, and we went onto the sacred burial grounds that had been preserved, thanks to archaeological work by Clifford and his team. We stopped at a large stone rock with a hole in it. He explained that this was considered a time portal by the ancient Hawaiians. The hole was a portal, called "The Leaping." I looked through the circular hole in the rock, about four inches in diameter, and the breeze shifted. I was transported back in time to ancient Hawaii, a time of mystical and complex thinking. Uncle Sam told me, "The female was the clear voice in the heavens, and the male was the man of the glad star of heaven. People listened to the ancient murmuring. Knowledge was passed from one Ulu to another Ulu. These were places of high learning, where the seven sacred teachings were taught. This was also happening simultaneously in Greece, and in aboriginal cultures like the Hopi, Blackfoot, Ojibway and others."

Little did I know that on my return to Vancouver, I would find an amazing story in the second journal about two noble royal Hawaiian ladies who spent several months aboard the *Discovery* for several months.

CHAPTER 24

The Second Journal

Tell the story, not the doctrine.

SAM KAHAʻI KAAI

Back in Vancouver, I returned to the Maritime Museum to continue reading Captain Vancouver's second journal. Here, there is the first hint of his independent thinking that would have disturbed the King and the Admiralty.

March, 1793 Karakaooa Bay, where Captain Cook fell. Yet to us it had produced an asylum, where the hospitable reception, and friendly treatment of such could not be surpassed by the most enlightened nation of the earth.

Captain Vancouver's sympathy and understanding for the indigenous people continues, throughout the journal. In addition, his respect and appreciation for them is evident in the tone of his entries.

The Captain had established a routine where he first met with the chief on board the *Discovery*, then went to shore, drew the line in the sand and reciprocal social relations were established, including Captain Vancouver's famous fireworks. (To this day, it is a tradition to have fireworks in Vancouver in the summer months.)

March 1793 The fame of our fireworks still attended us, and Trytooboory was very solicitous to be indulged with a sight of their effect. Considering that the present moment afforded no ill timed opportunity to impress the minds of these people more deeply with our superiority, his curiosity was gratified in the evening, by the display of a small assortment, from the after part of the ship. These were beheld by the surrounding natives with more than the usual mixture of the passions already described; for, on the present occasion they were regarded with a degree of awful surprise, that I had not before observed. This exhibition being finished, Trytooboory was conveyed into his canoe, in the same manner as he had entered the ship.

In the afternoon, our very attentive and useful friend Tomohomoha, having executed all his commissions, and rendered us every service and assistance in his power, bade us farewell. On this occasion I presented him with such an assortment of articles as afforded him the highest satisfaction. Of these, he was richly deserving, from the uniformity and integrity of conduct that he had supported from the first to the last moment of his being with us.

The few inhabitants who visited us from the village, earnestly entreated our anchoring, and told us, that if we could stay until the morning, their chief would be on board with a number of hogs and vegetables, but that he could not visit us then because the day was taboo-poory.

A canoe visited us that proved to be without exception, the finest canoe we had seen amongst the islands. The vessel was sixty one and a half feet long, exceeding, by four feet and a half, the largest canoes of Owhyee. Its depth and width were in proportion of building, and the whole of the workmanship was finished in a very masterly manner. The size of this canoe was not its only curiosity, the wood of which it was formed was made out of an exceedingly fine pine tree.

As this species of timber is not the produce of any of these islands, and as the natives informed us it is drifted by the ocean, it is probably the growth of some of the northern parts of America... The natives converted the tree into this canoe, which, by the lightness of its timber, and the large outrigger it is capable of supporting, is rendered very lively in the sea, and well adapted to the service it generally performs—that of communicating intelligence to Taio, whilst he is absent from the government of his own dominions.

The circumstance of fir timber being drifted on the northern tides of these islands is by no means uncommon, especially at Attowai.

Wade had extensive oral knowledge about the Hawaiians and

their visits to North America. "There was a whole mountain-side in Washington State allocated for the Hawaiians when they would visit the northwest coast. The Hawaiians knew how to sail to there, and they had maps on scrolls showing navigation routes. They were very knowledgeable about the islands and navigation in the Pacific. The ancestors knew how to navigate over millennia. They had expertise at reading the currents, they knew what the taste of the water meant, they could read the stars, the tides and the winds."

CHAPTER 25

The Jenny and Princess Raheina

Such was the deportment of these two women towards
us, by which they gained the regard and good wishes of,
I believe, everyone on board, whilst I became in no small
degree, solicitous for their future prosperity and happiness.

CAPTAIN VANCOUVER

alfway through the second journal, I came upon an amazing story. By this time, I had just about given up hope of finding anything about Lt. Baker, when this narrative began to unfold before my eyes. There were several pages of detailed descriptions of how Captain Vancouver handled two personal matters, one of two young royal Hawaiian ladies found aboard a boat called *The Jenny*, and the other when he mediates a personal relationship situation between King Kamehameha I and his Queen.

March 1793 Stories were circulated about two young women having been brought and disposed of by Mr. Baker, commanding the *Jenny* of Bristol.

I asked Lea Edgar if she had any information about a ship called the *Jenny* when I next visited the Vancouver Maritime Museum. She said she would look into it, but she had no luck. So I then emailed Judy Thompson in Victoria, explaining that Wade and I would be visiting Victoria the last week of June for some events, as Wade was a Director on the Board for Aboriginal Tourism BC. I asked Judy if she could look into the Maritime Museum records to see if there was anything about a boat called the *Jenny*.

Judy came by our information booth at the Royal Victoria Museum on Friday afternoon, June 20, with an air of excitement.

"Mary, I just could not believe it when I went to the file," she said. "There was an envelope in our files labelled: JENNY: THE SECOND SHIP INTO THE COLUMBIA RIVER, EMPTY 4/21/94. The contents were missing! Yet, whoever had taken the papers had left the envelope. So, no one has looked into this for 20 years!"

Is it possible that someone had attempted to cover up the purpose of the *Jenny*'s voyage? We knew the *Jenny* had been commanded by a Captain James Baker from Bristol. Lt. Baker's father, from Bristol, was also called James. It appeared that the *Jenny* was in both Hawaii and Nootka at the same time as the Vancouver expedition.

The Bakers of Bristol were a merchant, seagoing family. Is it possible then, that Lt. Joseph Baker's father was the captain of the *Jenny*, and would occasionally meet up with the *Chatham* and the *Discovery* on the voyages for trading purposes?

I continued reading Captain Vancouver's words, completely transported by the story of the two young Hawaiian women who were discovered on board the *Jenny*. I was on the *Discovery*, in Captain Vancouver's cabin, seated at his table. He interviewed all the persons in this drama, carefully listening to each version of the story in a reasonable and diplomatic manner. The two women were transferred from the *Jenny* to the *Discovery* in October, 1793, and Captain Vancouver details the story at length in his journal entries for March, 1793.

March, 1793 Although I had not any personal knowledge of Mr. Baker previous to his entering Nootka, yet I should conceive him totally incapable of such an act of barbarity and injustice; and if there was the least sincerity in the solicitude he expressed to me for the future happiness and welfare of these young women, it is impossible he could ever have meditated such a design.

I do not, however, mean to vindicate the propriety of Mr. Baker's conduct in bringing these girls from their native country, for I am decidedly of the opinion that it was highly improper, and if the young women are to be credited, their detention on board Mr. Baker's vessel were inexcusable.

They report that they went on board with several others of their countrywomen who were permitted to return again to shore; but that they were confined down in the cabin until the vessel sailed, and they were some distance from Onehow.

On the other hand, Mr. Baker states that he put to sea without any knowledge of their being on board his vessel.

But be that as it may, we found them thus situated at Nootka, and the future objects of Mr. Baker's voyage, leading him wide of the Sandwich Islands, he requested, as I then noticed, that I would allow them to take their passage thither on board the *Discovery*. To this I assented, and on sailing from Nootka, they were sent on board, and taken under my protection.

The names of these unfortunate females were Taheeopiah, and Tymarow, both of the island of Onehow. The former, about 15 years of age, was there of some consequence. The latter, about four or five years older, was related to the former, but was not of equal rank on the island.

Taheeopiah, for some reason I never could understand, altered her name to that of Raheina, a short time after she came on board, and was continued to be so called.

After leaving Nootka, our visit to the Spanish settlements, especially during the first part of our residence there, afforded them some recompense for the long and tedious voyage they had been compelled to undertake from their native country.

The sight of horses, cattle, and other animals, with a variety of objects to which they were entire strangers, produced in them the highest entertainment: and without the least hesitation or alarm, they were placed on horseback on their first landing, and with a man to lead the animal, they rode without fear, and were by that means enabled to partake of all the civilities and diversions which our Spanish friends so obligingly offered and provided. on all these occasions, they were treated with the greatest kindness and attention by the ladies and gentlemen; at which they were not less delighted, than they were surprised at the social manner in which both sexes live, according to the custom of most civilized nations, differing so very materially from that of their own.

These pleasures, however, they enjoyed but for a short time, for soon after our arrival at Monterrey, they were both taken extremely ill; and notwithstanding that every means in our power was resorted to for the re-establishment of their health, they did not perfectly recover until after our arrival at Owhyhee.

They seemed much pleased with the European fashions, and in conforming to this new system of manners, they conducted themselves in company with a degree of propriety beyond all expectation. Their European dress contributed most probably to this effect, and produced, particularly in Raheina, a degree of personal delicacy that was conspicuous on many occasions. This dress was a riding habit, as being best calculated for their situation, and indeed vested in our power to procure. Its skirt, or lower part, was soon found to be intended as much for concealment as for warmth; and in the course of a very short time, she became so perfectly familiar to its use in this respect, that in going up and down the ladders, that communicate with the different parts of the ship, she would take as much care not to expose her ankles, as if she had even educated by the most rigid governess; and as this was particularly observable in the conduct of Raheina, it is probable that her youth rendered her more susceptible of fresh notions, and of receiving new ideas and impressions from the surrounding objects, than the more matured age of her friend Tymarow.

The elegance of Raheina's figure, the regularity and softness of her features, and the delicacy which she naturally possessed, gave her a superiority in point of personal accomplishments over the generality of her sex amongst the Sandwich Islanders; in addition to which, her sensibility and turn of mind, her sweetness of temper and complacency of manners, were beyond anything that could have been expected of her birth, or native education; so that if it were fair to judge of the dispositions of a whole nation from the qualities of these two women, it would seem that they are endued with much affection and tenderness. At least, such was their deportment towards us; by which they gained the regard, and good wishes of, I believe, everyone on board, whilst I became in no small degree, solicitous for their future prosperity and happiness.

When Wade and I met with Clifford Naeole on December 19, 2014, at The Ritz-Carlton hotel, he explained that "Raheina" would be pronounced "Lahaina" in the Hawaiian language. This would make Lahaina a very high ranked princess, likely promised to an old chief. Was she a stubborn and highborn princess, who wanted no part of an arranged marriage? If so, could she have paddled out to the *Jenny* with her lady-in-waiting, and asked for asylum. Wade feels that the two royal women may have been promised to a rival chief as additional wives. They very likely did not want to marry these chiefs, and paddled out to the boat to escape severe punishment from their families, because this was against protocol. However, this is one interpretation.

The Baker family may have let them on the *Jenny*, which may have been the family's merchant ship, to protect them. Is it possible that James Baker had a kind heart and, having had conversations with his son Joseph (who would have been familiar with the chiefs and their entourages from his visits to the islands) allowed them on board before sailing for Nootka?

Uncle Sam, when told about this story on April 11, 2015, suggested that only a very highborn princess would have paddled out to a ship and asked for asylum.

Raheina was very likely born in Lahaina near the sacred healing stone. High princesses have 'dominion' (authority, power) Uncle Sam explained. The story was slanted by the Admiralty that these were just servant dancing girls or slave girls. This was untrue. Lahaina was the seat of the royal kingdom in Maui at one time. Uncle Sam later told us the history.

"Lahaina was originally called Malu Ulu Olele, the place of abundance and higher learning. The explorers called it the Venice of the Pacific. The late 1800s, the plantations changed everything and the birds stopped singing No one wrote down what really happened. Very few people know that Laheina means 'unmerciful sun.'"

Wade did some research when he was in Maui, and found out there was a sacred site on the east side of present-day Lahaina. There was a huge freshwater pond there, where a sacred dragon lived, and it was reserved for the nobility to cleanse themselves. The pool has long since been filled in, and is now the site of the Alano Club and the Holy Innocents Church. However, a map at the club still details the original sacred site.

ON JANUARY 27, 2015, after a meeting with Prof. Jack Lohman at the Royal BC Museum in Victoria, Judy Thompson invited me to the Maritime Museum to view the fourth journal, a detailed book of maps by Lt. Baker, which Judy had just uncovered in a dusty corner in storage. She carefully laid the book of maps on the table. I pulled on the white museum gloves, and started turning the pages, amazed at the beautiful, artistic detailing of Lt. Baker's drawings. In some cases, entire forests were drawn in precise and painstaking detail.

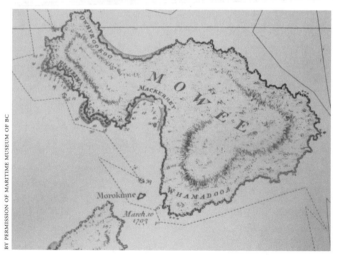

Map of Mowee (Maui) by Lt. Joseph Baker, March 1793

"When you last looked at the three volumes of Vancouver's voyage journals, the fourth volume was missing. We have now found it with our chart collection. It is a large folio with fold-out charts. Each one of them is labelled as prepared by Lt. Joseph Baker under the direction of Captain Vancouver. They are a reprint of the originals from the early 1800s," Judy told me. We were very excited, and wondered if these maps were the book of Baker drawings that Victoria had mentioned to me at the Lahaina Restoration Society offices .

On close inspection with a magnifying glass, Judy and I noticed that it is quite apparent that the *Discovery* anchored several times in "Raheina," which is the exact location of the present-day Lahaina in Maui. Also, the same map shows the island of Lanai labelled as "Ranai."

Learning about the *Jenny* brought back oral storytelling memories for Wade. "I remember the Lewis family, related to us through the Baker side, had a boat called the *Jenny*. They seemed to revere that name, as they mentioned it often. My Dad's boat was the *Godwood*.

"They all loved to sail, and would be gone for the fishing season for the summer runs to Knights Inlet, Kingcome Inlet and Johnstone Straits where the salmon came through. That is how they met their wives, from up north, Kwakiutl women. I cannot recall exactly which one of them owned the *Jenny*."

AFTER THE INCIDENT with the two royal women, Captain Vancouver refers to his mapmaker as "Mr." rather than "Lieutenant" Baker in the rest of his journal entries. It appears they become confidants as the captain asks Lieutenant Baker to bring in the *Discovery* to the Admiralty in Britain at the end of the voyage.

Wade feels it is very likely that Joseph Baker stayed on in the area of what is now Vancouver for a few months to gather furs from the summer to the fall. It is also very likely that furs were taken back to England by the *Jenny*, commanded by a member of Lt. Baker's extended family intermittently during the early voyages.

The lieutenant would have needed to be "family" to gain access to the hunting grounds. He would also have been able to continue his detailed mapping and drawings. According to oral stories, Lt. Baker had children with Kwasan, then more with her half-sister after Kwasan either died from pneumonia or left to go to the United States when she thought Baker would not return.

Is it possible that when he came each summer to Vancouver in June and July on the annual route from Hawaii to San Francisco (Monterrey) to Nootka, he stayed on, and then caught up with his shipmates in the Sandwich Islands in January on board the *Jenny*, which picked him up from Vancouver?

Lt. Baker seemed to have a great deal of freedom, and the dates certainly coincide with the oral history of him being in the Stanley Park area from July 1792 for several months, then returning to Hawaii, then proceeding to Nootka.

On April 14th, 2015, Judy Thompson from the Maritime Museum in Victoria sent us an email:

"Even better news! I was looking at photos of the *Chatham* and there is a photo labelled HMS CHATHAM AND THE JENNY, which I am attaching (copied from a 35mm slide). At last, the *Jenny*!"

The mysterious boat, the *Jenny*, had been found.

HMS Chatham and the Jenny, Baker's Bay, Columbia River, from a painting by H.R. Jackson

CHAPTER 26

Wymea, 1793

> *Treat this subject respectfully… you are writing*
> *history from the Royal Hawaiian point of view.*
>
> SAM KAHAʻI KAAI

I continued reading the story of Raheina and Tymarow. I realized that I just needed to be a scribe of Captain Vancouver's original words, not an author, as this amazing story unfolded.

March, 1793, The Sandwich Islands I was engaged on shore most of the day, in regulating a comfortable establishment that I had procured from the chiefs, for our two female passengers, the one named Raheina, the other Tymarow, who we had met with us already as stated at Nootka, in October 1792, and had brought them from thence, to restore them to this their native country; from which they had been forcibly taken and had endured an uncomfortable absence of a year. This office of humanity, to which their behaviour and amiable dispositions so justly entitled them, I was fortunate enough to accomplish to their satisfaction; and I had the pleasure of finding that they both acknowledged this, and the civil, and attentive treatment they had each received from every person on board the *Discovery* and *Chatham* with expressions of gratitude, and the most affectionate regard."

Onehow being their place of birth and former residence, I had promised to let them on shore on that island; but on our arrival at Owhyhee, I had understood that the inhabitants of Onehow had almost entirely abandoned it, inconsequence of the excessive drought that had prevailed during the last summer. Which had nearly caused the total destruction of all its vegetable productions. Finding on my arrival at Attowai [Hawaii] this information to be well grounded, I came to a determination to leave our female friends at this island.

Being well aware that the mode of living they had lately been constrained to adopt, and their having eaten at mine and other tables in the company of men, was an offense of so heinous a nature against their laws as to subject them both to the punishment of death, I took much pains to point out to Titeeree and Taio their innocence in this respect: and obtained from them both the strongest assurances, that they should not be liable to the least injury on that account, but that on their landing they should be immediately taken care of and protected.

These intreaties I enforced with Enemo, in the presence of Raheina and Tymarow when he was on board;

and had the satisfaction of receiving from him similar assurances of his protection; not only of their persons, but their property; and that whatever articles we might think proper to give them, should be secured to them, and no one should be permitted to wrest or extort any thing from them. These assurances being given not only by Enemo, but by the rest of the chiefs then present, I thought, by the purchase of a house and a small portion of land, to add to their future respectability and comfort.

This Enemo would not permit me to do, but instantly directed Oeashew to allot to each of them an estate in his newly acquired district of Whymea; to which Oeashew with much apparent pleasure consented.

The better to make sure of this donation, and to secure the permanent possession of it to these young women, I desired that the houses and land might be given to me, that the property should be considered as vested in me, and that no person whatever should have any right in it, but by my permission, and that I would allow Raheina and Tymarow to live upon the estates.

Matters having been in this manner arranged, Oeashew had gone ashore in the morning to fix upon the lands that were to be thus disposed of; and about three in the afternoon he returned, saying that he had fixed upon two very eligible situations adjoining each other, which I approved should be mine; if not, I was at liberty to make choice of any other part of the district I might think proper. In consequence of this offer, I attended him on shore, accompanied by some of the officers and our two females, who had received such an assortment of articles from us, as were deemed sufficient to make them respectable, without exciting the envy of the chiefs or their neighbours.

We found the situation proposed by Oeashew to be a very large portion of the fertile valley, noticed on our former visit on the western side of the river, commencing at the sea beach, and extending along the banks of the river to a certain established landmark, including a very considerable extent of the inland mountainous country. The contiguity of these estates to the commerce of the Europeans who visit this island, and the territory which it comprehended, was in value so far above our most sanguine expectations, that I was led to suspect the sincerity of the intended donation. But to this we became reconciled, from the protestations of the Chief himself, as also from the universal declarations of the natives who accompanied us, and who asserted that Oeashew really intended thus to dispose of the land in question. To which he added the most solemn assurances that he would protect them in the possession of it, together with their canoes, and all the articles they had brought with them from the ship, which declarations seemed perfectly to satisfy the young women, that they would be put into possession of their estates, and that their persons and property would be protected according to the assurances we had now received,

A long established line of division, formed by trees and a common road, separated the two estates. The lower one nearest the sea, which was the most extensive, was allotted to Raheina, the other to Tymarow, each of which they respectively took possession of, and in the warmest and most grateful terms acknowledged the obligations they were now under, for this last mark of our attention to their future happiness; and for the friendship and kindness they had experienced during their residence amongst us. They attended us to the beach, where they took an affectionate leave, and we embarked for the ship, leaving them to meditate on their new situation, and the various turns of fortune that had conspired to place them in such comfortable circumstances.

I enforced treaties with Chief Enemo, that the two ladies be treated in a respectful fashion. I was worried that they would be subject to death with their laws, Having eaten at mine and other tables in the company of men was taboo.

And, I purchased the two estates for them in my name in Whymea.[Hawaii]

On my arrival on board, I found our friend who had been employed in procuring us supplies, had returned with little success. seventeen middling sized hogs, a few potatoes, and some taro, without any yams, was the whole amount of their collection. our stock of water was completely replenished, and being satisfied from the report of the chiefs that no additional quantity of provisions was to be had at this island, I informed them that we should depart at the earliest opportunity. They inquired if I intended to visit the north side, as Poorey and Too would in that case continue on board for the purpose of assisting us in procuring some yams, which they said were more plentiful there than on the south side of the island.; but as nothing less than a very tempting opportunity would have induced me to go thither, I declined giving them further trouble, and having presented them with such articles as their services and the occasion demanded, they took their leave, with expressions of the highest satisfaction, promising to pay every attention, and afford all possible assistance and protection to their countrywomen whom we had just landed, and in whose future happiness and welfare they knew we had great interest.

Sketch of encampments at Atooi (Kauai) by J. Sykes, from the fourth journal

In addition to assisting the two royal women to find independence and security, Captain Vancouver also intervened in a personal argument between King Kamehameha I and his Queen in January and February 1794.

I told Uncle Sam about the intervention and counselling advice Captain Vancouver gave King Kamehameha and his wife when they were having relationship issues.

"Oh, she was a lot of trouble, that woman. She went into battle on the shoulders of a warrior," he said.

I also asked him about the spelling "Tameyamen" in the journals.

"That was K. The English couldn't say our K, they thought it was a T!"

Early in 1794, Captain Vancouver's very strong friendship with the King of Hawaii becomes apparent by a very touching story he describes about an argument between the king and his sacred wife, Queen Ka'humanu, and his intervention. I was told by Uncle Sam that this was highly unusual, and would never have been allowed previously, to allow a foreigner to intervene in a private matter. He explained that Queen Ka'humanu was seen before birth as being extraordinary and was given the name meaning "The Feather Cape." This was a name usually only reserved for men.

January, 1794 It appears that the infidelity of the queen had been rumoured, and when I enquired about the course of her absence, I had the mortification of understanding that there was a separation… I created a plan in my mind to bring about a reconciliation… The King always attended our meals, and in particular, he enjoyed breakfasts with us at the table.

February, 1794 I invited the Queen on board the *Discovery* for the purpose of presenting her with some trivial matters. I then arranged that the King would appear on board in a hasty manner, as if he had something extraordinary to communicate… I was arranging an accidental meeting, and hoped this would bring the reconciliation to pass without the least difficulty or explanation. The Queen and her entourage arrived first, then the King. I caught his hand, and joining it with the Queen, their reconciliations was instantly completed. This was fully demonstrated by the tears that involuntarily flowed down both cheeks as they embraced each other, and this produced such a happy circumstance that every individual present testified. A little refreshment from a few glasses of wine, concluded the scene of this successful meeting.

My interference was frequently solicited by them, and I used my best endeavours to bring about a reconciliation.

March, 1793 We took our departure from the Sandwich Islands, on Saturday the 30th of March, with the trade wind blowing principally from the North-northeast, and northeast, accompanied by very pleasant weather.

THESE TWO FASCINATING events, the story of Raheina and Tymarow and the intervention with King Kamehameha, show absolutely Captain Vancouver's character. He was a fair, compassionate commander who acted at the highest level. He did not listen to rumour or innuendo, interviewing all parties and negotiating with all concerned so everyone would feel comfortable. His language is far beyond the stereotype of the curt, brusque commander of the day. He also details places, people and events without judgement or prejudice. He was most concerned for the native's future prosperity, happiness and well being. This is before the advent of Darwinism, yet certainly Discovery Doctrine was already in effect. This makes Captain Vancouver's respectful approach all the more remarkable.

The Lords of the Admiralty in England, on reading or hearing about this, would have been very disturbed. Their intentions were the opposite: they had no interest in the future prosperity of the property, persons and and happiness of the indigenous people. In fact, they were likely working on a blueprint to dislocate the people from their lands.

Captain Vancouver, and likely Joseph Baker as well, had a very high level understanding of protocol, and the emotional subtexts of protocol. Captain Vancouver set a tone of caring about the wellbeing of the people they met on their travels. This had started with the Captain Cook episode, when he and Captain Clerke pacified the situation with the future king and the kahunas, which allowed Captain Cook to have a high chief's cremation funeral.

CHAPTER 27

The Third Journal

*The music and singing was by no means discord-
ant, or unpleasing; many of the actions seemed to
be well adapted, and the attitudes exhibited both
taste and elegance...*

CAPTAIN GEORGE VANCOUVER

Toward the end of his voyage of discovery, in the third volume of his journal, Captain Vancouver's entries show that the social interaction between the Europeans and the indigenous people were almost daily, cordial and respectful.

February, 1794, The Sandwich Islands The evenings were generally closed with singing and dancing, and the nights were as quiet as the most orderly towns in Europe, though it was a late hour most commonly when they retired to rest. The space between sunset and that time was employed by some parties in social conversation, and by others at various games of chance;

and I did not observe a single instance in which these were conducted, even by the losers, but with the greatest temper and good humour.

… I attended some of their evening amusements in our neighbourhood. At one, in particular, I was very well entertained. This was a performance by a single young woman of the name of Puckoo, whose person and manners were both very agreeable. Her dress, notwithstanding the heat of the weather, consisted of an immense quantity of thin cloth, which was wound around her waist, and extended as low as her knees. This was plaited in such a manner as to give a pretty effect to the variegated pattern of the cloth, and was other ways disposed with great taste. Her head and neck were decorated with wreaths of black, red and yellow feathers, but excepting these she wore no dress from the waist upwards. Her ankles, and nearly half way up her legs, were decorated with several folds of cloth, widening upwards, so that the upper parts extended from the leg at least four inches all round; this was encompassed by a piece of net work, wrought very close, from the meshes of which were hung the small teeth of dogs, giving this part of her dress the appearance of an ornamented funnel. On her wrists she wore bracelets made of the tusks from the largest hogs. These were highly polished, and fixed close together in a ring, the concave sides of the tusks being outwards; and their ends reduced to a uniform length, curving naturally each way from the centre, were by no means destitute of ornamental effect.

Thus equipped, her appearance on the stage, before she uttered a single word, excited considerable applause from the numerous spectators, who observed the greatest good order and decorum. In her performance, which was in the open air, she was accompanied by two men, who were seated on the ground in the character of musicians. Their instruments were both alike, and were made of the outsides of shells or large gourds, the lower ends ground perfectly flat, and as thin as possible, without endangering their splitting. These were struck on the ground, covered with a small quantity of dried grass, and in the interval between each stroke, they beat with their hands and fingers on the sides of their instruments, to accompany their vocal exertions, which with the various motions of their hands and body, and the vivacity of their countenances, plainly demonstrated the interest they had, not only in excelling in their own parts, but also in the applause which the lady acquired by her performance, advancing or retreating from the musicians a few short steps in various directions, as the nature of the subject, and the numerous gestures and motions of her person demanded. Her speech, or poem, was first began in a slow, and somewhat solemn manner, and gradually became energetic, probably as the subject matter became interesting; until at length, like a true actress, the liveliness of her imagination produced a vociferous oration, accompanied by violent emotions. These were received with shouts of great applause, and although we were not sufficiently acquainted with the language to comprehend the subject, we could not help being pleased in a high degree with the performance. The music and singing was by no means discordant or unpleasing; many of the actions seemed to be well adapted, and the attitudes exhibited both taste and elegance.

This is in direct contrast to later descriptions by missionaries, referred to by 20th-century historical and government texts, with their political and religious biases. These took one sentence or observation out of the context of dozens of pages of positive descriptions of the local people.

February, 1794 The satisfaction we derived at this public entertainment, was greatly increased by the respectful reception we met from all parties, as well performers and spectators, who appeared to be infinitely more delighted by our plaudits, than by the liberal donations which we made on the occasion.

These amusements had hither been confined to such limited performances, but this afternoon was to be dedicated to one of a more splendid nature, in which some ladies of consequence, attendants on the court of Tamaahmaah, were to perform the principal parts. Great pains had been taken, and they had gone through many private rehearsals, in order that the exhibition this evening might be worthy of the public attention; on the conclusion of which I purposed by a display of fireworks, to make a return for the entertainment they had afforded us.

About four o clock, we were informed it was time

to attend the royal dames; their theatre, or place of exhibition was about a mile to the southward of our tents, in a small square, surrounded by houses and sheltered by trees. A situation as well chosen for the performance as for the accommodation of the spectators, who on a moderate computation, could not be estimated at less than four thousand, of all ranks and descriptions of persons.

Those who had been successful in their commercial transactions with us, did not fail to appear in the best apparel that could be procured, and such as were destitute of European articles, had exerted their genius to substitute the manufacture and productions of their own country in the most fashionable and advantageous manner. Feathured ruffs, or bartering tape in wreaths, adorned the ladies heads, and were also worn as necklaces; red cloth, printed linen, or that of their own manufacture, constituted the lower garment, which extended from the waist to the knees. The men likewise had put on their best maros; for that the whole presented a very gay and lively spectacle.

On our arrival, some of our friends were pleased to be a little jocular with our appearance at so unfashionable an hour. Having come much too early for the representation. But as we were admitted into the green room amongst the performers, our time was not unpleasantly engaged. The dress of the actresses was something like that worn by Puckoo, though made of superior materials, and disposed with more taste and elegance. A very considerable quantity of their finest cloth was prepared for the occasion; of this their lower garment was formed, which extended from their waist half way down their legs, and was so plaited as to appear vey much like a hoop petticoat. This seemed the most difficult part of their dress to adjust, for Tamaahmaah who was considered to be a profound critic, was frequently appealed to by the women, and his directions were implicitly followed in many little alterations.

The play was in honour of a captive princess, being held about fifty miles away, called Crycowculleneaow.

March, *1794* On our arrival at the place of exhibition, we found the performers assembled, consisting of a numerous throng, chiefly of women who were dressed in their various coloured clothes, disposed with a good effect. The entertainment consisted of three parts, and was performed by three different parties, consisting of about 200 women in each, who ranged themselves in 5 or 6 rows, not standing up, or kneeling, but rather sitting upon their haunches. One man only advanced to a few feet before the centre of the front row of ladies, who seemed to be the hero of the piece. He gave tone and action to the entertainment. In this situation and posture, they exhibited a variety of gestures, almost incredible for the human body so circumstances to perform. The whole of this numerous group was in such perfect unison of voice and action, that it were impossible, even to the bend of a finger, to have discerned the least variation. Their voices were melodious… they exhibited great ease and much elegance, and the whole was executed with a degree of correctness not easily to be imagined. This was particularly striking in one part, where the performance instantly changed from a loud full chorus, and vast agitation in the countenances and gestures of the actors, to the most profound silence and composure; and instead of continuing in their previous erect attitude, all fell down as if lifeless, and in their fall buried themselves under their garments; conveying in some measure, the idea of a boisterous ocean, becoming suddenly tranquillized by an instant calm. The great diversity of their figured dresses on this occasion had a particularly good effect… It was conducted through every part with great life and vivacity, and was without exception, the most pleasing amusement of the kind we had seen performed in the course of the voyage.

Captain Vancouver once again makes a brief mention of the incident of the Jenny, in this very interesting excerpt.

March, 1974 The *Jenny* was a very small three masted schooner that had visited Nootka in October1792, commanded by Mr. Baker, who had proceeded in her to England,with the cargo of furs he had then collected. (In 1794, she was then commanded by a Mr. John Adamton, who had returned with her from England.) The story had acquired some degree of credit with Señor Quadra and the rest of the Spanish Officers who had heard it. The arrival of the *Jenny*, however, in the port of Nootka, gave a flat contradiction to these scandalous reports, and proved them to be equally malicious and untrue; as the two girls were found still remaining on board the *Jenny*, without having entertained any idea that they were intended to be sold, nor did they mention to have received any ill usage from Mr. Baker, but on the contrary they had been treated with every kindness and attention while under his protection."

He also mentions returning to the island of Hawaii to "meet with the two young women again at their Whymea Bay estates" to ensure their well being.

CHAPTER 28

Willful Blindness

Captain Vancouver was a good, correct career
officer, and he crossed the wrong group of people.

ANONYMOUS VANCOUVER MUSEUM SOURCE

My research and reading of the Captain Vancouver journals made me very frustrated. How could historians have missed these pages and pages of references to the local inhabitants? Originally, I thought I would only find one or two brief references. But there were so many that I had to write down every one, word for word, because I thought it was the only way we would be believed.

My PhD friend Sarah took pity on me, and took me to the museum staff lunchroom one day for a jolt of strong coffee. "They do not usually ever allow us in here, but I have been here so long researching that they occasionally allow me to make a coffee," she said with a smile, brushing her long hair from her face.

Sarah advised me, "You need to be careful listening or reading stories that may have been slanted or biased to discredit

Captain Vancouver's reputation in the very class-conscious England of the time."

I realized that not one single official history text I had seen described Captain Vancouver visiting the native villages, socializing with them, conducting firework displays, etc. Either no one had read these journals, which was difficult to believe, or the Discovery Doctrine was so ingrained in the collective colonial consciousness that a type of willful blindness to the actual and very active social engagement occurred. In addition, not one single mainstream history book had been written from the indigenous perspective, other than the dozens of books on First Nations' legends and myths, or stories about reserve life, which one native friend calls the "dead, dying or crying stories."

These stereotypes are still written into the textbooks and, in our opinion, damage the self esteem of the young native students who come across them in the mandatory Socials 10 and 11 courses. I can hear Captain Vancouver whispering across the centuries, telling me to set the record straight. At the end of the voyage, he handed HMS *Discovery* over to Lt. Baker, and instructed him to return the ship in to England in September 1795. Did Captain Vancouver anticipate the cold reception he would receive? Is this where Joseph Baker is leading us, and is this why the Captain confided in Lt. Baker, and handed him the ship and papers rather than presenting them himself to the Admiralty, which was normal protocol?

Wade and I believe Captain Vancouver did not have the heart to deal with them, and went home in silence, hoping to preserve some of his personal journals.

Reading the journals, it is apparent that everywhere they

went, they would land and pitch tents or stay in the village homes of the chiefs. Strong friendships were made, some of the officers had relationships with the daughters of chiefs and kings. Children were born. On the positive side, Wade believes that these children would have inherited a strong immunity against European diseases from their British fathers.

The system of status and rank would have mutually encouraged relationships between naval officers, Hudson Bay Post managers and superior chiefs' daughters. Up until the Indian Act of 1876, this was certainly the case. Then in the later decades of the 19th century, the arrival of prejudiced American gold miners, who came with a slave trading mentality, poisoned the atmosphere and contributed to the creation of the Indian Act.

I decided I needed to go back to the journals to see if Captain Vancouver had any thoughts about these matters. He was politically very astute and aware. In his third journal, he discusses in length his political views, and the disingenuous method of justifying colonial takeover.

February, 1794 I was well persuaded that they had just cause to complain; particularly the fraudulent and deceitful manner in which the traffic with the natives had been conducted.

In many instances, no compensation whatever had been given by these *civilized* visitors, after having been fully supplied, on promise of making an ample return, with the several refreshments of the very best quality the country afforded. At other times, they had imposed upon the inhabitants, by paying them in commodities of no service or value, defects which were undetectable on first examination by the natives. This was more particularly the case in those articles which they were most eager to obtain, and most desirous to possess, namely, arms and ammunition; which chiefly composed the merchandise of the North West American adventurers. muskets and pistols were thus exchanged that burst on being discharged the first time, though with the proper loading. To augment the quantity of gunpowder which was sold, it was mixed with an equal, if not a larger proportion of pounded charcoal. Several of these fire arms, and some of the powder, were produced for my inspection in this shameful state, and with the hope that I was able to afford them redress.

Many very bad accidents had happened by the bursting of these firearms. In one case, a very fine active young chief had lately purchased a musket, and on his trying its effect, lost the fingers of his left hand, and his right arm below the elbow....had it not been for the timely assistance of some of our gentlemen, his life would have been in imminent danger.

When these people are given imperfect and insufficient conditions for a valuable consideration, it is not only fraudulent but barbarous and inhuman. notwithstanding which, should these inhabitants resort to measures of revenge for the injuries thus sustained from the Northwest American adventurers, they would immediately be stigmatized with the epithets of savages and barbarians, by the very people who had been the original cause of the violence they might think themselves justified in committing.

Under a conviction of the importance of these islands to Great Britain, in the event of an extension of her commerce over the pacific ocean, and in return for the essential services we had derived from the excellent productions of the country, and the ready assistance of its inhabitants, I lost no opportunity for encouraging their friendly dispositions towards us; notwithstanding the disappointments they had met from traders, for whose conduct I could invent no apology; endeavouring to impress them with the idea, that, on submitting to the authority and protection of a superior power, they might reasonably expect they would in future be less liable to such abuses.

The long continued practice of civilized nations, of claiming the sovereignty and territorial rights of newly discovered countries, had heretofore been assumed in consequence only of priority of seeing, or of visiting such parts of the earth as were unknown before; but in the case of Nootka, a material alteration had taken place, and great stress had been laid on the cession that Maquinna was stated to have made of the village and friendly cove to Señor Martinez

Notwithstanding that on the principles of the usage above stated, no dispute could have arisen as to the priority of the claim that England had to the Sandwich Islands; yet I considered that the voluntary resignation of these territories, by the formal surrender of their King and the people to the power and authority of

Great Britain, might probably be the means of establishing an incontrovertible right, and of preventing any altercation with other states hereafter.

Under these impressions, and on due consideration of all circumstances, I felt it an incumbent duty to accept for the Crown of Great Britain the proceeded cession, and I had therefore stipulated it be made in the most unequivocal and public manner.

For this purpose all the principal chiefs had been summoned from the different parts of the island, and most of them had long since arrived in our neighbourhood.

They had all become extremely well satisfied with the treatment they had received from us, and were highly sensible of the advantages they derived from our introducing amongst them only such things as were instrumental to their comfort, instead of warlike stores and implements, which only contributed to strengthening the animosities that existed between one island and another, and enabled the turbulent and ambitious chiefs to become formidable to the ruling power.

They seemed in a great measure to comprehend the nature of our employment...which under my command acted under the authority of a benevolent monarch whose chief object was to render them more peaceable in their intercourse with each other, to furnish them with such things as could contribute to make them a happier people, and to afford them an opportunity of becoming more respectable in the eyes of foreign visitors.

I recollected that my own counsel and advice had always been directed to exhort them to a forgiveness of past injuries and proving to them how much their real happiness depended upon a strict adherence to the rules of good fellowship towards each other, and the laws of hospitality towards all such strangers as might visit their shores. I had endeavoured to adopt conciliatory measures, after having convinced my aversion to wicked or unworthy persons, this was consistent with my duty as a man, and with the station I then filled.

March, *1794* There were now 11 white men on the island: but excepting Young and Davis and Boid, I much fear that our Owhyhean friends will have little reason to rejoice in any advantages they will receive from their new *civilized* companions.

In the spring, Captain Vancouver and his crew returned to the west coast of Canada.

April, *1794* The young Chief Chatidoolz possessed a great authority. Some of our gentlemen, in quest of game on shore, had fallen in with a family of about 18 natives from whom they received the kindest attention and civility, and they had in return invited a few of them on board, which they readily accepted. After a hearty supper of salt meat and biscuit, they rested very quietly until the next morning.

July, *1794* We received dispatch of declaration of

war against England, and the death of Louis XVI and anarchy in France…

Seven hundred canoes, 9 Russians. There were 1400 Kodiak Natives in Cook's Inlet…

[Meeting a Kwakiutl Chieftain] His robe was of mountain sheep, and the headdress of bright copper and brass plates, from which hung a number of tails or streamers of wool and fur. The whole exhibited a magnificent appearance.

August, *1794* The unjustifiable conduct of the traders on this coast, has enraged the inhabitants, and is what has caused them to attempt acts of hostility.

CHAPTER 29

The Lords of the Admiralty

*In the end, the establishment formed ranks and
ostracized Captain Vancouver.*

DR. NIGEL RIGBY, HEAD OF RESEARCH,

NATIONAL MARITIME MUSEUM, GREENWICH, ENGLAND

I was sitting at the Salish Sea gathering event on August
10, 2014 at my booth with some presentation material
about *The Hidden Journals*. I was enjoying the warm
breezes from the ocean and listening to InterTribal, a young
hip hop couple, who were performing nearby.

I looked up from my reading, and there was a salty old
seaman standing in front of me. He had noticed the historical posters presenting information about Lt. Joseph Baker
and Chief George Capilano's daughter. We started chatting,
and I told him about this book, still in the research phase.
The seaman pulled out an old book from under his jacket—
Northwest Explorations by Gordon Speck—and gave it to me.

"Here. Read this," he said.

"How will I get it back to you?" I asked.

"Give me a copy of *The Hidden Journals* for it," he replied, with an amused smile. Then he disappeared.

I began to read his gift to me.

Those who have studied Vancouver as a man over-emphasize his harshness and pride, those who write of him as an explorer permit his feats of exploration to excuse obvious character weaknesses. The ones who berate him accuse him of using cruel and unusual punishments for the slightest infractions of orders... They point out that the lash was ever around Vancouver's wrist, ready to be laid on bare backs; that he had no use for or sympathy with anyone's ideas but his own, and that a broken head or dank days in the ship's dungeon were the penalties for voicing opposing views. [12]

What a different picture of the man that was revealed by our research! Throughout his journals, his respect and sympathy for the indigenous people he encountered shines through, both in the Sandwich Islands and in the Pacific Northwest. Captain Vancouver, and likely Joseph Baker as well, had a very high level understanding of protocol and its emotional subtexts. Captain Vancouver set a tone of caring about the wellbeing of the people they met on their travels, as evidenced, for example, by his treatment of Raheina and her companion.

Our research indicates that on his return to England, and even before, there was a campaign by the Lords of the Admiralty to discredit him. The publication of Archibald Menzies's 1791 letters to Joseph Banks were early precursors to what would become a campaign to discredit Vancouver, before and after his return to England. Sir Joseph Banks was an English naturalist, botanist and patron of the natural sciences. He was president of the British Royal Society and and a trustee of the British museum for 42 years. He was in charge of the "official" accounts of voyages, and he was an advocate for colonization in the new territories. Young Mr. Pitt (later Lord Camelford), the prime minister's nephew, was sent home by Captain Vancouver in disgrace from the *Discovery*, and this routine ship discipline issue was blown out of proportion.

It is very apparent that the Lords of the Admiralty were quite concerned about what may be in the journals of the Discovery from July 1795 on, and it appears that Mr. Menzies had been asked to keep notes in addition to the botanical ones. At any rate, there was definitely consternation about documents aboard the Discovery in the final leg of the Voyage.

He was starting to be painted as a touchy and temperamental commander who not only needed to be restrained from undoing the work of his botanist Menzies, but whose actions were generally unpredictable... Before the expedition had even left England, ill feeling openly flared because of a misunderstanding as to Menzies' rights in the mess. Letters back to Joseph Banks, his patron, from Menzies show a petulant and easily offended man working hard to paint Captain Vancouver in an unfavourable light. [13]

This is quite the opposite of what I had read in Captain Vancouver's journals, which show a fair and temperate man. When he returned to Britain, he asked Joseph Baker to return the ship and the documents to the Admiralty. He decided to go home for a few days. Why? In my opinion, he knew that his findings about the indigenous kingdoms were not following the dogma of the day, and it was not in his heart to hear the reprimands.

Wade and I discussed these writings with Sam Kaha'i Kaai. He commented, "Captain Cook's journals were not esteemed in England, and Captain Vancouver's books were destroyed or disappeared… his family, the church and the Admiralty would have been horrified at the time about what he was saying. It would have been considered blasphemous."

The Lords of the Admiralty closed ranks on Captain Vancouver to the point that he was ridiculed in newspaper cartoons, and it was unsafe for him to walk the streets. He died just under three years later, even though he came home in perfect health (according to the last pages of his journals), contrary to official documents of the time which said he was in ill health.

There is a hand-coloured etching in the National Portrait Gallery in London, England, called "The Caning in Conduit Street." The cartoon, by James Gillray, was published in the newspapers on October 1, 1796, and shows Thomas Pitt, 2nd Baron Camelford, and another man attacking Captain Vancouver, with while two onlookers laugh in the background. This would have been highly embarrassing to the very correct and protocol-conscious Captain Vancouver.

I recalled saying to Sarah one day in the Vancouver Maritime Museum, as we were sitting companionably at the large mahogany research table. "It is hard to believe that a teenage boy —Thomas Pitt—could have been the source of Captain Vancouver's downfall, as mainstream historians seem to think."

"Not without help," she said astutely.

From his journal entries, it appears that he realized the native peoples were superior in many ways than to the so called "civilized nations." This is why he would have run into the roadblocks on returning to London.

Wade and I believed that Captain Vancouver's original journals had disappeared, and the edited versions had been rewritten and interpreted because his clearly expressed opinions ran counter to the political agenda of the British imperial powers and subsequent colonial generations.

Support for our beliefs came from an unexpected source in February, 2015, when I had a fascinating transatlantic conversation with Dr. Nigel Rigby, Head of Research at the National Maritime Museum in London, England. Roy Clare, Director of the Auckland Museum in New Zealand, and a former Rear Admiral, had recommended that I speak with Dr. Rigby.

I asked Dr. Rigby about the missing journals of Captain Vancouver.

"The theory is they went missing somewhere between the Lords, the printers and the Channel Islands. The trouble is, no one really knows for sure. I assume the last time they were seen was likely by his brother, John Vancouver. I have never seen any references. It is unusual. Even his alleged portrait, the one with the raised eyebrow in the National Portrait gallery, has no artist's name, and no name of the sitter. I also don't recall any mention of a relationship between Lt. Joseph Baker and Captain Vancouver.

"In the end, the establishment formed ranks and ostracized Captain Vancouver. It was a real hatchet job."

I asked Dr. Rigby if he had any idea how it was done. Would it have been an open discussion in the House of Parliament?

"Probably not," Dr. Rigby said. "It was a small community of the elite at the time, lots of social events at the clubs and country houses. It was done with little notes. I have seen them from Lady Camelford and others, saying things like 'May I call on you tomorrow?' Lord Camelford ultimately came out quite well. Although my feeling is he was balmy. He was writing letters to his mum and by the end of his time on the ship, they were just scrawls.

"One of the criticisms of Captain Vancouver was that he had the Pitt boy (later Lord Camelford) flogged with a cat o'nine tails leather whip, a method of severe punishment. I have seen the note stating this. However, it was not signed and then went missing."

"Could the note have been fabricated?" I asked Dr. Rigby.

"Possibly, " he said. "Captain Vancouver was quite sparing with the whip, he was no brute. Lt. Baker would report to him about any discipline issues, and then he would hear the for-and-against before deciding."

"That is my feeling, as well, from the research." I said.

I asked Dr. Rigby about his thoughts on Captain Vancouver.

"I feel he was quite a careful man, and perhaps lost his temper under stress. I have seen writings that say he was ill, perhaps a thyroid problem."

Our research, I related to Dr. Rigby, revealed that Captain Vancouver and his men came back in 1795 in perfect health. "Our Hawaiian oral historians believed that he became ill and died from emotional stress and a broken heart after being excluded and bullied on his return to England."

"That is an interesting perspective, one I have not heard before," Dr. Rigby said. "I have seen writings in the history books that Captain Vancouver was not of the gentry and that his officers were. Class was all important in those days. However, in my personal opinion, I rather think it was the opposite. I think that Captain Vancouver was the snob. Most of the studies I have seen are of the ship, rather than the person."

I agreed that, judging from his prestigious court style of writing, it is apparent that Captain Vancouver had been highly educated and was comfortable with people he considered had the same social status as himself, such as the kings and superior chiefs he met on his voyages.

I also asked Dr. Rigby if he had come across any material about relationships between the officers and the royal ladies. "It was not uncommon," he answered. "The Pacific had that reputation. It was perfectly natural."

Judy Thompson at the Maritime Museum obtained some information for us about the Lords of the Admiralty. The Lord High Admiralty of England was an office first established in 1391 when Edward, Earl of Rutland, was appointed Admiral of England, uniting the offices of Admiral of the North and Admiral of the South. Commissioners were first appointed in 1628. Many of the successive First Lords were serving naval officers. All were members of Parliament, either of the House of Lords, or of the Commons, and were thus responsible to the Parliament as well as to the Sovereign, for all aspects of naval command and administration. The

Lords Commissioners ceased to exist in 1964 when the three separate service Ministries were brought together in a single Ministry of Defence. The title, though not the office, of Lord High Admiral, was then resumed by the Crown in the person of Elizabeth II.

Further research on the Discovery Doctrine, the Monroe Doctrine of 1823 and Terra Nullius was enlightening.

The Discovery Doctrine is based on 14th-century laws, also called the Papal Bulls, where lands not occupied by Christians were deemed vacant. The law was based on the advocacy of Catholic popes at the time (*Summa Theologica*, 1271) "that unbelievers deserve not only to be separated from the Church, but also to be exterminated from the world by death." This was reaffirmed in the following centuries; the tribes that occupied the land were, at the moment of discovery, no longer completely sovereign, and had no property rights, but rather merely held a right of occupancy. This became law in 1608 in Britain. Further, only the discovering nation, or its successor, could take possession of the land from the natives by conquest or purchase. These laws stayed embedded in the consciousness of colonial nation for centuries, and were used to justify heinous acts of torture, murder and conquest.

The Monroe Doctrine was buried in a routine annual message delivered to Congress by President James Monroe in 1823. It warns European Nations that the United States will not tolerate further colonization. It proclaimed the right of the United States to have international police powers in all matters in the Western Hemisphere. From that point on, the United States ordered marines to keep Europeans at bay and to maintain control of the indigenous people and others.

Terra Nullius is a Latin expression deriving from Roman law meaning "nobody's land," which is used in international law to describe territory which has never been subject to the sovereignty of any state, or over which any prior sovereign has expressly or implicitly relinquished sovereignty. In August 1835, Governor Bourke of New South Wales, Australia, implemented the doctrine of Terra Nullius by proclaiming that indigenous Australians could not sell or assign land, nor could an individual person or group acquire it, other than through distribution by the Crown. This reinforced the notion that the land belonged to no one prior to the British Crown taking possession. By 1992, Terra Nullius was the only justification for the British settlement of Australia.

"Historians, more interested in politics than archives, misled the legal profession into believing that a phrase no one had heard of a few years before was the very basis of our statehood," according to the historian, Michael Connor.[14] These laws have still not been repudiated, and many feel they are the reason that Australia, New Zealand, Canada and the United States did not sign on to the United Nation's international rights of the indigenous people charter in 2007. Canada finally signed the document on November 12, 2014, however, insists that this does not change Canadian laws.

"The Discovery Doctrine has been severely condemned as socially unjust, racist, and in violation of basic and fundamental human rights."[15]

Then, in 1858, Darwin published his theory of evolution, a natural selection process based on the survival of the fittest. Indirectly, it changed many minds about making treaties with indigenous nations. On his deathbed, Darwin recanted some of his theories, but it was too late. Very conveniently, Darwin's expedition was sent out from 1831 to 1836, and interestingly, that is when the stories about the indigenous people start to change. It appears that it is was not in the best interests of the Crown to present the indigenous people in a positive light starting from the early 1830s, so they needed material to contradict the previous respectful and positive stories coming back from the explorers. They found justification in Darwin's writings.

In 1856, the British established the colony of British Columbia on the mainland, with a colonial proclamation vesting all land with the Crown. In 1876, the Canadian government created The Indian Act, which removed the indigenous people forcefully from their lands and placed them on reserves. This outdated Indian Act is still in effect today, even though later social anthropologists like Franz Boas had completely different theories.

An article published in the *Times Colonist* newspaper, on February 21, 2015, states:

> *Canada's Truth and Reconciliation Commission is weighing whether to ask the Vatican to repeal the Papal Bulls of Discovery that granted 15th century explorers the right to conquer the New World and the "heathen" aboriginals who called it home.*
>
> *Chairman Murray Sinclair says the commission examining the impact of Canada's Indian Residential Schools*

is looking carefully at the 1455 and 1493 Catholic edicts as part of its final report.

Many argue the proclamations legitimized the treatment of aboriginals as "less than human". Crown sovereignty in Canada can be traced back to those Papal Bulls and neither Canada nor the United States has repudiated them, Sinclair said.

The movement to repudiation is very strong and is moving ahead, Sinclair said in an interview. If we as the commission are going to join that movement or endorse it.. we have to come to a conclusion that it is necessary for reconciliation, to establish a proper relationship between aboriginal and non-aboriginal peoples.

I thought about the great harm that these Doctrines had caused, and I imagined a scene at one of London, England's exclusive private clubs in 1796.

THE CARRIAGE STOPPED in front of the Brooks's Club on Pall Mall, in the St. James's area of London. Lady Camelford and her son stepped into the freezing cold rain and entered the club by the side door. They briefly nodded to the hall porter as their coats were taken.

"Good evening, m'lord," the hall porter said. "Welcome to Brooks's."

He glanced at Lady Camelford with disdain, privately thinking that the members should never have made an exception to allow certain highborn married (or widowed) ladies to enter the club for the biannual Prime Minister's dinner. The porter watched them walk down the hall and up the grand staircase into the Subscription dining room, where Joseph Banks and Prime Minister William Pitt were already holding court. And it was Joseph Banks whom Lady Camelford particularly wished to meet.

Lord and Lady Camelford were greeted warmly and shown to their seats. They enjoyed a very fine meal, with the best wines in London, as Brooks was famous for its cellar. Several waiters attended them throughout the dinner. Lady Camelford waited until the main meal was finished, and looked for an opportunity to speak privately to Joseph Banks. She found her chance when he left to go to the privy. She quietly excused herself and waited discreetly in the dim, candlelit hallway, adjusting her bodice and smoothing her hair at one of the large antique mirrors on the wall. She was pleased by her reflection in the mirror. She saw Banks returning and approached him.

"May I speak with you for a moment on a private matter?"

"Of course," he said.

"You realize my son Thomas is now Lord Camelford, due to my late husband's early and unfortunate passing. He is now one of the youngest members of the House of Lords," she said haughtily.

"George Vancouver put my son off his ship to the Daedalus in 1793, and makes no mention of my son in his journals, as if he was an insignificant nuisance teenager. Yet he talks for pages and pages about 'royal ladies' he meets on those little islands, as if they were our equals!

"He has also feigned no interest in meeting with me to discuss this since his return, and he does not return my calling cards."

"My dear Lady Camelford, I fully appreciate how distressing this must be for your family," replied Banks. "I have heard rumours from my good friend, Archibald Menzies, about some possible mistreatment. All fairly routine for a ship, but we can certainly put a different slant on the matter if needed.

"His journals did not quite take the direction we had hoped, and this situation needs to be carefully managed." He lowered his voice.

"The British press is always ready to spread some ridicule on our behalf if needed. I will speak to our portrait artist, he is quite good with caricatures. A discreet campaign of shunning may be needed to remove any influence he may have. In the meantime, keep that boy of yours under control. Perhaps you can ship him off to the West Indies?"

Lady Camelford said. "May I send you my *visite bilete* [calling card] by my footman next week to discuss the matter further? We can meet in the morning room."

"Yes, of course," Banks said. "I am obliged, I cannot encourage what I disapprove of so highly."

They returned separately to the dining table, and discussions resumed.

"Some members of the House are becoming entirely too soft on the slave trade, and on the local natives. We will have to send out another expedition to discredit some of these stories of inappropriate relationships from Cook, Vancouver and the French ships. Of course, we can expect it from the French," said Lord Brooksbank. Everyone around the table had an amused laugh.

"We have to put a stop to all this. It will jeopardize our Doctrine of Discovery laws, our land policies abroad and disrupt our social orders. We will be having some meetings with the Bishops. This all has to be carefully and discreetly managed. Perhaps another expedition? One to demonstrate that the natives in these new lands have no permanent rights? And we need to diminish the roles of these so-called chiefs and kings. Only our church can place a crown."

"People are starting to feel the need to take sides. I have heard whispers from some of the reformers that this could be considered nothing but piracy. Look at what is happening in France, complete anarchy. We have to prove that these people of the land are not stewards of the land, just transitory occupants. Some of these explorer journals need to disappear from public view."

"Our duty is clear, we need to maintain the colonies for the glory of Great Britain and the Crown."

A chorus of hear-hear resounded around the table.

"Let us retire for our cognacs," Lord Brooksbank said. He looked pointedly at Lady Camelford.

She said to her son. "We should be leaving now, and leave the men to their talks. I am not feeling well."

Thomas called the carriage, and escorted his mother home.

W. KAYE LAMB, in his edited version of the journals, discusses the final years of Captain Vancouver's life.

The harassment continued with unfounded and manufactured charges of mutiny until George Vancouver dies in early May 1798, a brief two and a half years after his return. No court of inquiry was ever convened…

The opinion was widely held that Camelford was deranged.

*His arrogance, bad temper and propensity for violence soon
ruined his prospects, and he died at 29 years old, March 11,
1804, after a pistol duel over an alleged insult.*[16]

Wade and I feel that Pitt was manipulated and exploited
by the establishment; it would have been a very easy matter
to have him stop harassing a significant man. We believe it
was all orchestrated by Lady Camelford, Joseph Banks and
others, because Captain Vancouver's journals described the
local kings and chiefs as sovereign equals, which contradicted
the Discovery Doctrine.

The later decades of the 18th century was a time of rev-
olution—the French and the American—and a new way of
thinking would have affected the young men on the voyages, mentored by enlightened and educated thinkers like
Captain Vancouver. King George III was considered mad,
and England was near bankruptcy at the time. It was not in
the interest of the Empire to treat indigenous peoples with
respect and allow them the right of sovereignty.

However, in 1795, Spain and Britain finalized agreements
at Nootka which ceded the coast to the British. Captain
Vancouver was no longer needed. He had very effectively
obtained the lands for Britain without any bloodshed. He
had served his purpose, and his reports that did not fit into
the new agenda were to be ignored.

Sept.12ᵗʰ, 1795
*Sir, I have received your Order of this day's date, address to
me as Surgeon of His Majesty's Sloop Discovery, demanding
my Journals, Charts, drawings etc of the Voyage, but I can*

assure you, that, in that capacity, I kept no other Journals than the Sick Book, which is ready to be delivered up if you think it necessary.

I perfectly recollect the orders of the Lords Commissioners of the Admiralty being read on the 2nd of July last, and also the conversation which I afterwards had with you, relative to the mode of conveying the Journals, Papers, Drawings, etc. in compliance with my Original Instructions, to the Secretary of State's office; but situated as I am at present I trust you are not insensible of the necessity which urges me to Act with more caution in this respect. I therefore beg leave to acquaint you that I do not conceive myself authorized to deliver up these Journals, etc to anyone till they are demanded of me by the Secretary of State for the home department, agreeable to the tenor of my Instructions, of which I believe you have a copy; if not, mine is at your perusal.

I am, Sir

Your most Obedt, Humble Servt

ARCHIBALD MENZIES [17]

THOUGH NOT YET forty years old, Vancouver was an old man, worn out with physical hardship and responsibility. Perhaps he had contacted tuberculosis. Whether or not that is true, certainly he was already a dying man when he retired from the navy and took a little place in Petersham to rest and write his memoirs.

Even in his few remaining years, he was constantly embroiled in personal quarrels, according to this book.

It is very interesting that in this book, there are virtually no letters or actual quotes from Captain Vancouver. All the material is from letters from Joseph Banks and Archibald Menzies.

One does not have to be Hercule Poirot to believe that this whole situation is set up to discredit Captain Vancouver. In our research, Captain Vancouver states that everyone on board the *Discovery* came back in perfect health from the voyages. He was very concerned about a healthy diet with meat and vegetables and fish. But Vancouver died just three short years after his return to Britain.

The Captain's report of the health of his crew appear at the end of his third journal.

September, 1795 From the first moment of my appointment, to the hour in which I resigned the station I had so long held, the health of every individual under my command had been my first care; and I had now the unspeakable happiness of beholding the same persons return on board the Discovery to the river Shannon, in perfect health, as had sailed with me from the River Thames.

By my list, it will appear that, from the 15th of December, in the year 1790, to this 13th day of September 1795, comprehending a space of four years, eight months and 29 days, we had lost out of our compliment of one hundred men, only one man by disease; and at the time of our parting with the *Chatham*, at St. Helena, she had not, in the course of the whole voyage, lost a single man, either in consequence of ill health, or form any accident whatever.

From the *Discovery*, only five men lost, mainly by accidental drowning.

The unfortunate loss of these five men, from the *Discovery* produced in me infinite regret, but when I adverted to the very dangerous service in which we had been so long employed, and the many perilous situations from which we had been providentially extricated, with all possible adoration, humility and gratitude, I offered up my infringed thanks to the GREAT DISPOSER OF ALL HUMAN EVENTS, for the protection which thus, in his unbounded wisdom and goodness, on all occasions, to vouchsafe unto us, and which had now happily restored us to our country, our families and friends.

After all our research it became apparent that a campaign of shunning has been in place for almost 200 years. The missing journals and documents, the absence of an official portrait of Captain Vancouver, the missing files on the *Jenny*, the slanted views in all mainstream history books, from which the Captain's voice is missing. Some voices carry through time and some have not. To ensure the Discovery Doctrine prevailed, the strongest voices echoing from the past are those of Sir Joseph Banks, Archibald Menzies, Lord and Lady Camelford and the British Establishment at the time. The following definition of 'shunning' shows what Captain Vancouver was subjected to:

Shunning can be the act of social rejection, or emotional distance… Social rejection occurs when a person or group deliberately avoids association with, and habitually keeps away from an individual or group. This can be a formal decision by a group, or a less formal group action which will spread to all members of the group as a form of solidarity. It is a sanction against association, often associated with religious groups and other tightly knit organizations and communities. Targets of shunning can include persons who have been labeled as apostates, whistleblowers, dissidents, strikebreakers, or anyone the group perceives as a threat or source of conflict. Social rejection has been established to cause psychological damage and has been categorized as torture or punishment... Social rejection has been and is a punishment used by many customary legal systems.[18]

It is time to bring forth the true voices of Captain Vancouver, Joseph Baker and the kings and chiefs they encountered on their voyages.

"The direct result of Captain Vancouver and the oral stories being lost are the residential schools, the Indian Act and what happened to my father Daniel and Uncle James. Learning the First Nations' Studies curriculum at the learning centre was a dismal experience and negatively affects the morale of many First Nations' students, leaving us in despair. This was the personal consequence to me of the rewriting, editing and hiding of information in the journals over that last 200 years, information that showed my ancestors in a positive light," said Wade.

Wade and I discussed this with our daughter, who was studying Frantz Fanon's book, *The Wretched of the Earth,* in one of her courses at the University of British Columbia. The book is about the dehumanizing effects of colonization upon the individual. Sierra was writing an essay on the book at the time, and she told us that the book states that "colonialism is a machine not capable of thinking."[19]

Something about the grand idea of colonialism warps a part of the human psyche, and allows it to become as mindless as naked violence. The goal becomes to hurt and oppress for the sake of superiority, and this is unjust. Essentially, people get rolled into one big, mindless mass, and it is unifying for them to be pitted against a nameless "other." [20]

Sierra told us she felt that a much stronger force is love and determination. Captain Vancouver humanized the people he was meeting, and loved them.

"Yes, Captain Vancouver's true voice was lost for political reasons," Wade said. "He was shunned and his actions questioned. The consequences of this cascaded down through history.

"It is very exciting to me to hear his true voice from the original journals and logbooks, and his bravery and courage in standing up to the Lords and others when he returned to England. He never disavowed his beliefs and findings from the voyages. Instead, he chose to live in privacy for the last short two and a half years of his life."

CHAPTER 30

A Visit from the Captain, 2014

Bring me to life and bring the discord to an end...
we loved and appreciated each other... standing
shoulder to shoulder with kings and chiefs..."

CAPTAIN VANCOUVER

Toward the end of 2014, I met with Kevin Miller, Director of Operations at the Renaissance Harbourside Hotel on West Hastings Street in Vancouver. We were talking about having a book launch there, and were sitting in the lobby lounge having Earl Grey tea together. Kevin was very interested in explorers and navigators, having just come back from a cruise to Alaska. He had been born in Liverpool, England, and we discussed at length how these men, at a young age, left England in search of unexplored lands and adventure. We both remarked on how it seemed as if historical books and movies had ended with Captain Cook.

The theme of the hotel is "Live Life to Discover," and the third-floor meeting rooms were named after various international ports—perfect for a book launch. Kevin asked me to do five historical posters for the elevators with the "Live Life to Discover" theme.

Kevin's cell phone rang, and he was called away to another meeting. I sat and finished my tea, and picked up my briefcase, about to leave the hotel. Something told me to take the elevators to take a look at the third-floor meeting rooms. A wealthy-looking matron rode in the elevator with me, and we both looked at the standard posters, promoting the restaurant "2B Bistro and Bar."

"It is very generic, isn't it? she commented.

"Yes," I replied. "I have been asked to look into the possibility of changing these to more of an explorer theme."

I got off the elevator, and looked at the silent meeting rooms, bearing names of ports of call from around the world. There was no one around, not even an errant waiter looking for a quiet corner to contemplate life.

I took the elevator back to the lobby, and I noticed a small sign next to the button for the second floor said "Port of Vancouver." Kevin had not mentioned the second floor. Something compelled me to take the elevator back up to the second floor. The doors opened, and I stepped out into a large space.

There was a mysterious feeling to this second floor. Again, there was no one there. I was alone in the large hall. I leaned my elbows on a tall desk, and looked out through the windows to Burrard Inlet and the North Shore mountains, thinking: This was a wonderful space for a meeting. The lights seemed to flicker, then dim. I saw candles in sconces on the walls.

FROM THE SHADOWS, he stepped out in front of me, about 15 feet away, respectfully keeping his distance. He did not come closer; the protocol had not yet been established. The line was drawn in the sand. He waited.

"Can you come closer, and tell me what you want me to say about you," I asked.

He came a few feet closer, and knelt in front of me, like a knight. He then stood up, and walked a few feet back and stood between the two columns. I stood with my back to the table.

"Bring me to life. Bring the discord to an end. We loved and appreciated each other, standing shoulder-to-shoulder with kings and chiefs.

"Tell them the truth about who we really were, not the misconceptions and disrespectful connotations put on our words and actions by men who never left their desks, private clubs and safe harbours. Tell them we sailed the oceans with all their myths and glory, and saw the rising and setting of the sun, and saw the magnificence of the colours and the peoples we met.

"Our words were altered or hidden when we returned. There is an injustice here, and you need to write about it, my dear friend.

"I have been busy visiting my friends for the last 200 or so years. However, now I am troubled by the way the world is turning. The young people have lost their way in dark rooms. They need to go out to sea and feel the wind on their faces, and feel the love of exploration and meeting strangers who become allies and friends."

"Why did you visit me now and not before?" I asked

the Captain. "I have been reading your words for the last several months."

BY PERMISSION OF THE ROYAL BC MUSEUM, VICTORIA, BC

Probably Captain Vancouver. Artist unknown

"Because I had to know you would stand up for me, that you were brave enough to do so," he replied. "Even though you know there are some people that do not want these matters known. They prefer the myth that we are all separate—a myth foisted on us by greedy land-herders, for whom no amount of land was enough. Dislocating the native people from their rightful places was their constant unending goal, passed from father to son.

"There will be those who will not believe what you are

writing. Do not concern yourself with them. Willful blindness was not just a disease in my time.

"Your world will not move forward until the conquerors make peaceful treaties with those of the land. They need to ask for reciprocal good tidings, good relations and warm welcomes in return, not the ranting of the disgruntled few."

Then he was gone. I tried to remember what he looked like, as there is no official portrait of Captain Vancouver. The shunning campaign by the Lords had resonated down through the ages.

All I can remember is that he was tall and well-built, not overly slender, and had an intelligent and worldly countenance.

I WAS AT the Vancouver Maritime Museum, for one of my biweekly research visits, and realized I felt very weary and tired. Sarah made me a coffee, and suggested we sit in the lounge. Her large dark eyes looked at me compassionately.

"The information coming to me about Captain Vancouver's discreditation in England when he returned is very upsetting," I explained to the sympathetic Sarah. I told her about the satirical cartoon I had seen, about how he could not walk the streets in peace, and about the shunning I was convinced had happened.

"You have definitely put a new perspective on the white, privileged western view of the world," Sarah said.

"The story I come across in museums and books always has the same timeline," I said. "1778: Captain Cook. 1778–1820: aggressive natives battling with explorers and each other.

1830: here come the missionaries and Darwin to 'civilize' the indigenous world."

"Yes, that sounds like the story told to the public," Sarah replied.

"Captain Vancouver did not fit the dogma of the time, so he was discredited," I suggested.

"The biographies I have read say that he was a good, correct career officer, but he then crossed the wrong group of people," Sarah told me.

I went on. "Imagine his emotional stress, feeling humiliated and discredited. He died three years after his return. It seems that there were the Captain Vancouver experts, and no one really questioned them. They perpetuated the myths fabricated by certain lords. I am trying to correct a distorted perspective of history."

Captain Vancouver's final words, at the end of his third journal:

September, 1795 Having communicated to Captain Essington such parts of my orders from the Lords of the Admiralty, under which I had sailed, as applied to the government of my conduct on the present occasion, I received his orders to repair immediately to London, and the following day, after having seen the Discovery safely moored, with the rest of the fleet, in the Shannon, and giving such instructions, as circumstances demanded to my first Lieutenant Mr. Baker, in whose zeal for service, and abilities as an officer, a long experience justified me in implicitly confiding, I resigned my command of the *Discovery* into his hands, and with such books, papers and charts as had been previously selected as being essential to the illustration of the services we had performed, I took leave of my officers and crew, not however, without emotions which, though natural, on parting with a society with whom I had lived for so long, shared so many dangers, and from whom I had received such essential services, are far more easily to be imagined than I have the power to describe, and in the course of a couple of days, I arrived at the Admiralty, where I deposited my several documents.

Before I bid farewell to the *Discovery* (Arrived all well in the Thames the 20th of Oct. 1795) I must beg leave to arrest the attention of my readers for a few minutes, for the purpose of taking a short view of the geographical knowledge which had been obtained of the earth, previously to the expedition which I have had the honour to command, and the happiness of bringing thus to a conclusion, and also to notice such parts of the globe yet remained to be explored to make that species of information complete.

The effecting of a passage into the oriental seas round the Cape of Good Hope, the discovery of America, and the opening of a communication between the Atlantic and Pacific oceans, by passing either through the Straits of Magellan, or round the islands lying off the southern extremity of Tierra del Fuego, engaged the minds and utmost exertions of the most illustrious navigators during the last three centuries. These enterprises have been duly appreciated and justly celebrated for the important lights they have thrown upon the sciences of geography and nautical astronomy, for the improvements they have caused in the arts; for the commercial intercourse which, by their means, has been opened and established with all the maritime parts of the world…

There were few objects to which I had paid more attention, or had more sincerely at heart, than that of observing such a conduct, at all times, towards the several tribes of Indians, with whom we should frequently meet, as should prevent the necessity of our resorting to any measures that might endanger the lives of a people, whose real intentions were always likely to be misunderstood, from a want of knowledge in us of their respective dialects or languages. After having resided, as it were, amongst them for more than two years, without having had the least occasion to fire a shot in anger…

CHAPTER 31

The Tall Ship Sail, August, 2014

The smells of the rigging and the ropes seemed familiar to me.

WADE BAKER

One hot August day, we drove down to Grays Harbour in Washington, and were let through the Peace Arch at the border by a dour customs agent, who was annoyed at me for leaving my sunglasses on. A passing tourist in Stanley Park had told us we must go to see the *Lady Washington*, a tall ship docked at Grays Harbour for only a couple of days.

We parked the car at the port and walked down the docks to the ship. We saw the tall masts swaying in the light breeze in the distance, as if a mirage had come to life. As I was climbing aboard, something suddenly made me greet the sailor on the deck with, "I am Wade Baker. May I have permission to board, Captain?" The words came out inexplicably.

MARY TASI

I felt I was stepping onto the path. I was feeling numb, not knowing the reality—is his world, Lt. Baker's, colliding with mine now?—almost to the point where I was going blank. It was too much to grasp.

The bronze-skinned seaman's eyes widened in surprise. "Sure, come aboard," he said.

I thought we would only be looking at the riggings, but

then Mary said, "I bought tickets. We are going for a two-hour sail."

I felt astonished and something blocked me for a few minutes. Mary became really upset with me, and walked off the ship, saying, "We are coming back and doing this!"

She said to me, "We are moving forward about this story. We need to be on this ship and feel what it was like so long ago. This is amazing that we were told by that American tourist to come here today. The ship is only here for the weekend."

The *Lady Washington* was built in Aberdeen, Washington, by the Grays Harbour Historical Seaport Authority. She is a full scale reproduction of the original *Lady Washington*, built in 1776, and named after Martha Washington.

As Mary walked off the ship, she said to the old seaman sitting outside, "He does not want to go for the sail." He just smiled at us.

We went into the village of Blaine, and had a wonderful authentic Mexican dinner with fish tacos and ice-cold, non-alcoholic beer with ice. I was now getting more excited, and feeling less numb.

We returned at the appointed time, and were collected with about 15 others by the young bosun.

"You are lucky" he said. We usually have over 50 people. Must be the long weekend—we have very few for the sail today."

We walked down the creaking dock and up the gangplank to the deck. A young Indonesian man with long braided hair down his back helped us over the deck.

To my astonishment, we were on a tall ship from the exact time period my forefather sailed. This was an eye-opening experience for me, to be in his realm on the high seas. What would it be like to venture where few Europeans had been before?

For the first half hour or so, I stood silently by the railings on the lower deck. However, I felt uncomfortable there. I pondered Joseph Baker walking these decks in the past; he would have likely visited the original of this ship. The smells of the rigging and the ropes seemed familiar to me.

MARY TASI

Suddenly, I found myself standing next to Captain Johann on the upper deck. This is where the Captain would bark out his orders to the officers, and they would then relay the messages to the rig-masters. I stood on his right side. This is where Joseph would place himself, where he could look over the crew, decking and rigging. It was a solemn feeling of the tasks at hand, where he would take the Captain's orders and relay them to the rigging masters to set certain protocols for the sails.

To my right side, against the side of the upper deck were the "Royals," the small, fast sails that Joseph Baker mentions often in his logbooks. The "Royals" were used when there were only very light breezes, and were put on the very top of the masts when the boat was hardly moving. I felt at ease in that spot, where I could oversee the crew. I felt that Joseph Baker was actually with me, happy to see I was the only one of his West Coast descendants to care about his place in those past times. It was exciting to be standing in his place, where his authority was respected.

"GRANDFATHER, THIS IS an interesting place to stand where you once stood. It makes me feel I am getting to know you better as a person of respect and honour, and the role you played on this *Discovery* journey of the Pacific West Coast."

Joseph Baker spoke to me. "This is the first time anyone has stood in my place of authority and respect. Know that you now have played a part of who I was: Third Lieutenant. I'm really grateful you have brought my story to the future, where I thought I would not be recognized, and sit in the legend of history and bring my story alive. I am an ocean-going person. I have been to many native lands and seen many cultures. I loved all the women I lived amongst. I lived my life with them, and I respected them and cared for their well-being. I lived life at the most, we all knew we could be lost at sea at anytime. It is a dangerous career."

"What happened when you went back to England," I asked him. "Did you return to visit us?"

"My voyages as a young man were over, and I felt the

loss of my adventures. I needed someone to console me. To live out my retirement and play the father role that I longed for and missed, and watch my grandchildren grow… Yes, I returned to see how my extended family were doing, and George Vancouver and I talked at the table about the trouble to come. That came true: the hardships for the people… I knew I left children there, more than one, son and daughter and more…

"I came to see how they were coming along. I always asked for more sea duty, until only a few short years before my death. It was great to see my blood living in this part of the world. I am sad I only had a moment with them. 'Go back home settle down and become an old man at the end.' Those were my orders."

TWO WEEKS LATER, Mary and I were in English Bay in Vancouver, sitting at some rocks at the shoreline to talk about the book. The warm sun felt good on my face, and I looked out into the Bay where my ancestor would have anchored, and walked on these shores with his native friends. I felt his presence again.

As we climbed up the rocks and left the ocean's shore at English Bay, I felt my Dad smiling at me and saying in jest, "Well, I am glad at least one family member is taking the time to write this down…"

Endnotes

1. Vancouver, George and John Vancouver (ed.). A *Voyage of Discovery to the North Pacific Ocean and Round the World, in which the Coast of North West America Has Been Carefully Examined and Accurately Surveyed: Undertaken by His Majesty's Command Principally with a View to Ascertain the Existence of Any Navigable Communication Between the North Pacific and North Atlantic Oceans, and Performed in the years 1790, 1791, 1792, 1793,1 794, & 1795 in the Discovery Sloop of War, and Armed Tender Chatham, Under the Command of Captain George Vancouver.* Paternoster Row, London: G. G. and J. Robinson, and J. Edwards, 1798

2. Fitzpatrick, Gary L. and Riley M. Moffat (contr.). *Early Mapping of Hawai'i.* Honolulu, HI: Editions Limited, 1987

3. Wing, Robert C. *Joseph Baker: Lieutenant on the Vancouver Expedition.* Seattle, WA: Gray Beard Publishing, 1992. p89

4. Tasi, Mary. *Spirit Memory.* North Vancouver, BC: Sky Spirit Studio Books, 2014. p45

5. Kelm, Mary-Ellen and Lorna Townsend (eds.). *In the Days of Our Grandmothers: A Reader in Aboriginal Women's History in Canada.* Toronto, ON: University of Toronto Press, 2006. p177

6. Pynn, Larry. "Mystery Man." *Vancouver Sun,* May 24, 2007

7. Kirkness, Verna (comp. & ed.). *Khot-La-Cha: The Autobiography of Chief Simon Baker.* Vancouver: Douglas & McIntryre, 1994

7. Kirkness, Verna (comp. & ed.). *Khot-La-Cha: The Autobiography of Chief Simon Baker.* Vancouver: Douglas & McIntryre, 1994

8. Ibid

9. Speck, Gordon. *Northwest Explorations.* Hillsboro, OR: Binford and Mort, 1954, p17

10. Rosecians, C.E. (ed.). *Hawaii's Young People Magazine,* April 1898

11. Ibid

12. Speck, p129

13. Speck, p147

14. Connor, Michael. "The Invention of Terra Nullius." *The Bulletin*, Sydney, Australia, August 20, 2005

15. Pagden, Anthony and Jeremy Lawrance (eds.). *Vitoria: Political Writings*. Cambridge: Cambridge University Press, 1991

16. Lamb, W. Kaye. *Voyage of George Vancouver 1791–1795*. London: The Hakluyt Society, 1984. p238

17. Speck. p148-149

18. https://en.wikipedia.org/wiki/Shunning, accessed September 3, 2015

19. Fanon, Franz. *The Wretched of the Earth*. New York, NY: Grove Press, 2005. p23

20. Ibid. p50

Bibliography

Andra-Warner, Elle. *Hudson Bay Company Adventures*. Victoria, BC: Heritage House Publishing, 2003

Armitage, Doreen. *Around the Sound*. Madeira Park, BC: Harbour House Publishing, 1997

Braden, Gregg. *Deep Truth*. New York: Hay House, Inc, 2011

Bridge, Kathyrn. *Voices of the Elders*. Victoria, BC: Heritage House Publishing, 2013

Kane, Herb Kawainui. *Ancient Hawai'i*: Honolulu, HI: The Kawainui Press, 1997

Kirkness, Verna (comp. & ed.). *Khot-La-Cha: The Autobiography of Chief Simon Baker*. Vancouver, BC: Douglas & McIntryre, 1994

Fisher, Robin. *From Maps to Metaphors: The Pacific World of George Vancouver*. Vancouver, BC: UBC Press, 1993

Fitzpatrick, Gary L. and Riley M. Moffat (contr.). *Early Mapping of Hawai'i*. Honolulu, HI: Editions Limited, 1987

Fanon, Franz. *The Wretched of the Earth*. New York, NY: Grove Press, 2005

Fournier, Suzanne. *Shore to Shore: The Art of Ts'uts'umutl Luke Marston*. Madeira Park, BC: Harbour Publishing, 2014

Gabaldon, Diana. *Lord John and the Private Matter*. Toronto, ON: Random House, 2003

Gough, Barry. *Juan de Fuca's Strait*. Madeira Park, BC: Harbour Publishing, 2012

Hull, Raymond, Gordon Soules and Christine Soules. *Vancouver's Past*. Vancouver, BC: Gordon Soules Economic and Marketing Research, 1974

Layland, Michael. *The Land of Heart's Delight*. Vaictoria, BC: TouchWood Editions, 2013

Lamb, W. Kaye. *Voyage of George Vancouver 1791–1795*. London: The Hakluyt Society, 1984

Liiliuokalani, *Hawaii's Story by Hawaii's Queen*. Honolulu, HI: Mutual Publishing, 1990

Lipton, Bruce, PhD. *The Biology of Belief*. Hay House Inc, 2005

McBride, Likeke R. *The Kahuna*. Hilo, HI: Petroglyph Press, 1972

Mullins, Joseph G. *Hawaiian Journey*. Honolulu, HI: Mutual Publishing, 1978

Nicol, Eric. *Vancouver: The Romance of Canadian Cities Series*. Toronto, ON: Doubleday Canada, 1970

Provenzano, Renata. *A Little Book of Aloha*. Honolulu, HI: Mutual Publishing, 2003

Rae, John. *Arctic Correspondence*. Victoria, BC: TouchWood Editions, 2014

Sinclair, Marjorie. *Nahi'ena'en*a. Honolulu, HI: Mutual Publishing, 1995

Speck, Gordon, *Northwest Explorations*. Hillsboro, OR: Binford and Mort, 1954

Stone, Irving. *The Origin*. New York, NY: Doubleday & Company Inc. 1980

Thompson, Eric S. *Maya Archaeologist*. Norman, OK: University of Oklahoma Press, 1963

Westervelt, W.D. *Myths and Legends of Hawaii*. Honolulu, HI: Mutual Publishing, 1987

Waite, Donald. *Vancouver Exposed*. Vancouver, BC: Waite Publishing, 2010

White, Ellen Emerson. *The Royal Diaries–Kaiulani, The People's Princess*. New York, NY: Scholastic Inc., 2001

Questions of Enquiry for Discussion

1. What examples of leadership can you find in this story?

2. Define Doctrine of Discovery. Find examples in the book, and from other research.

3. What is critical thinking? Explain how you think critical thinking is explored in this story.

4. Why do you think Captain Vancouver was shunned when he returned to England in 1795?

5. How did Captain Vancouver maintain such strong and friendly relations with the local people he met? Why do you think he felt it was important? Why do you think he may have supported an alliance marriage? Why do you think Chief Capilano may have supported an alliance marriage?

6. Discuss examples of the protocols that were followed around trading.

7. Discuss discipline methods on the ships, and compare to discipline methods today.

8. Why do you think King Kamehameha I was called 'The Lonely One'? What qualities make a good leader?

9. Why do you think some history books do not describe the high level and respectful relationships between the explorers and the local indigenous people? How do they describe them? Give examples. Compare with examples from this book.

10. Explain what Ho'oponopono means. Find an example in the book.

11. Why do you think Captain Vancouver's original hand-written journals are missing?

12. Why do you think the English government of the time edited the journals?

13. How would you explore your family history? Where would you start? Would you use oral history or written history. Discuss the difference between the two.

14. What does Captain Vancouver mean by "office of humanity"?

15. What is the Coast Salish native name for Mount Baker?

About the Authors

Wade Baker and his wife and partner Mary Tasi founded Sky Spirit Studio in 1995, the year of their daughter Sierra's birth. Wade is a sculptor, graphic designer and red cedar carver. He has been carving and creating art since he was a teenager. As a descendent of ancient Coast Salish, Kwakiutl, Tlingit and Haida nobility, Wade has inherited a rich artistic legacy. In these traditions, art is not a separate activity, but is interwoven in life, language, custom and culture. Art is a means of spiritual expression in which a design or piece of art can encompass an entire story. From his British ancestors, he has inherited a love of exploration, particularly in visiting and learning about other cultures.

Wade's preference is to create large public art sculptures. He has worked in steel, wood, glass, marble and many other mediums. His stainless steel "North Star" was commissioned for the 2010 Olympics and stands at the Vancouver Olympic Village site. One of the highlights for Wade was meeting Prince Charles when the North Star was unveiled in 2009.

Wade has also produced smaller public art designs, and in 2000 Wade's wolf design was selected to be part of the millennium series of Royal Canadian Mint quarters. Fifty million quarters were produced with Wade's design and are now in circulation.

Wade is a member of the North Vancouver Chamber of Commerce, and a Director at Large for Aboriginal Tourism British Columbia.

MARY TASI IS an art consultant, urban designer and writer. She worked for many years in Ontario and Quebec as an urban planner and designer. She is a member of the Canadian Institute of Planners, the Planning Institute of British Columbia and the North Vancouver Chamber of Commerce.

Mary's philosophy is that art brings community together to develop new ideas. A highlight was working with the City of North Vancouver and the Squamish Nation to create the "Gateway to Ancient Wisdom" for the beginning of the North Shore Spirit Trail. This public art piece brought together elders, youth, landscape architects, builders, contractors, steel workers, welders, politicians and many others in an innovative, award-winning collaborative process.

Mary and Wade established the publishing house, Sky Spirit Studio Books, in 2014.

Books may be ordered through the website:
www.skyspiritstudio.com
Or through Red Tuque Books:
www.redtuquebooks.ca

Wade Baker and Mary Tasi are available for presentations and workshops. For more information, contact:
info@skyspiritstudio.com